The
Ethics of
Smuggling

The Ethics of Smuggling

by BROTHER ANDREW

with a Foreword by CORRIE TEN BOOM

Tyndale House Publishers, Inc. Wheaton, Illinois

Library of Congress
Catalog Card Number 74-80770
ISBN 8423-0730-3
Copyright © 1974
Tyndale House Publishers, Inc.
Wheaton, Illinois
Tenth printing, October 1979
Printed in the
United States of America

CONTENTS

FOREWORD

There is always a special place in my heart for my so much younger brother, Andrew. And I think the reason is that he is doing so much that I would have liked to do. But when he asked me if I would write a Foreword for this book, my first thought was: what can I say about a book with a title like *The Ethics of Smuggling?*

I know that Brother Andrew doesn't like the word "smuggling," nor do many of his readers. And neither do I. I learned, at the beginning of my work for the Lord, to pray for everything, and some years after the war I bought some new watches in Switzerland and put them in my suitcase. As soon as I was in my seat on the plane, I prayed for the crew, the passengers, and the person sitting next to me, and then I started to pray: . . . and Lord, will you just help me to sm - - - -.

I could not say it. And that very moment I learned that I could not ask the Lord for something that was against his will. Do you know, I was glad to pay the import duty?

Some time ago, I was speaking in a church in the American South. It was a large church, but there were still many young people sitting on the blue carpeting. I love to see the faces of the listeners when I tell about the Lord, and that night the lighting in the church made it possible for me to see a great many.

One of the stories I told them was of the red suitcase full of Bibles that I took into Russia. Yes, I prayed for those Bibles very much. I even asked the Lord to send angels to protect the Bibles. And he did. It always makes me happy to tell that story, but when I looked at some of the faces of those listening, I knew something was wrong.

Whenever I'm asked to speak I always have a vertical connection with the Lord, as well as the horizontal one with the people. So I asked him, what was the matter? He showed me that in the eyes of many, smuggling is sin, and that is all there is to it.

But he also gave me another story which helped those who were troubled. During the Nazi occupation of Holland, my family and I were involved in saving Jews. One day we learned that all the babies in a Jewish orphanage in Amsterdam were about to be killed. Though I knew it was against the law of that time to interfere, I also knew we had to do something for those little ones.

I talked with the young people who were working with us, and they worked out a plan to save the babies. That same day, the boys in our group "stole" them, and the girls took them and knocked on many doors, and how happy we were that so many arms opened to receive those frightened little bundles of humanity!

Thy word have I hid in mine heart, that I might not sin against thee (Psalm 119:11). What may we do as Christians to make this verse real to people all over the world? We Christians are one Body, and as Watchman Nee said, "When my feet were whipped, my hands suffered pain."

Are your hands suffering? In many parts of the world there are people who have never seen a Bible, or read one verse of Scripture. I am so thankful for the brave young people who are not afraid to give up their lives to go to those places where the fields are not yet yellow for the harvest, but where some of them look black — ready for the seed.

And they overcame him by the blood of the Lamb, and by the word of their testimony; and they loved not their lives unto the death (Revelation 12:11).

Corrie ten Boom

INTRODUCTION

During a campaign I was having somewhere in South Africa, a man rushed up to me with a letter at the beginning of a meeting. I just had time before the message to open the letter and to read this:

> "Paul, writing to the Romans, says that governments are put in authority by God for the maintenance of law and order."

Then there were three questions:

> 1. "Is the Communist government put in authority by God?"
> 2. "Were other totalitarian governments—for example, Hitler's and the Roman Empire's—placed by God?"
> 3. "Can a Christian criticize his government when it goes against the Word of God?"

As I read those three questions, I was startled. Suddenly I realized that this whole issue of Bible-smuggling, which some people regard as an ethical issue, is basically a matter of knowing whom to obey and recognizing where we stand.

Right then in the message, as I was speaking on the Great Commission, I was able to give the answer to that gentleman who had written those three questions to me.

Because certain Christians debate the morality of what we are doing in our ministries, I want to state my convictions quite frankly. The Lord has mightily demonstrated to me and my fellow-workers that it is his will for this work to continue. At the same time, of course, I confess that I expect some critics to remain unconvinced. People who tell me that I am doing something wrong have not convinced me, nor have I persuaded them to change their minds. Even factual information will not budge certain fixed opinions.

When my earlier book, *God's Smuggler*, appeared, I admit that I wasn't completely happy with that title. Like many other people, I associated bad things with smuggling, such as narcotics or slaves. Besides that, it implies the negative idea of breaking the law. But the word has stuck, and so I am stuck with it. It surely has caused some wild notions about what we do. We are not some kind of spiritual stunt men who go careening recklessly around eastern Europe in our little station wagons full of Bibles trying to see how much we can get away with and not get caught. The plight of our persecuted brethren is far too desperate for us to pull tricks just for the fun of showing off.

Not of this world
What we really are is special agents of a Government not of this world. We do everything we can to promote the cause of our sovereign Lord,

whether we are allowed to do it in the open or are forced to do it under cover. Perhaps the whole thing is redeemed by being linked with God: if indeed I am a smuggler, it is to do God's work among God's people with God's supplies and according to God's orders. Actually, labels make little difference. What matters is that we obey the Lord.

The things that I discuss here will mean the most to Christians who are hard at work for Christ in their own places of assignment, and who therefore long to hear about the prospering of his cause elsewhere. Such brothers and sisters will take courage from the evidence in our mission that God's promises can be trusted totally, despite criticism from our friends and determined opposition from the enemy. We do what we do in the way we do it because we believe with all our hearts that it is right for us before the Lord. No Christian should serve Christ on any other basis.

In these years that we have been taking Bibles into eastern Europe, a lot of controversy has developed in certain Christian circles about such "smuggling." Naturally, in the very character of such a work, there is bound to be some mystery, and consequently some misunderstanding. It is difficult, if not impossible, to explain everything about a mission that requires a degree of secrecy in order to survive and function effectively. We respect the earnestness of many of the critics, and commend the good works that they are doing for Christ as they are led by the Holy Spirit.

Now, however, the time has come for me to make as clear as possible the principles upon which our work is based, with the hope that God will use our example to stir his people to more aggressive and imaginative action against the forces of the Evil One that would try to block the spread of the gospel.

Marching
Orders

Imagine that you are a soldier whose commanding officer has ordered you to invade enemy-held territory. You plan your attack to catch the opposition off guard by striking when and where he least expects it. But as you move forward, you discover that his fortifications are well constructed. What's worse, he must have learned your plan, or else his sentries saw you coming, for suddenly his guns open fire and you are blasted into retreat.

You report back to headquarters, and your officer asks: "Well, did you capture that position?"

"No, sir," you reply. "The enemy won't let me."

Do you think you would get away with that? That isn't what warfare is all about. When a soldier receives an order, he is bound by his oath of allegiance to fight to the death to fulfill it. He won't let himself be stopped simply because the enemy is entrenched and armed to resist. He knows that fact even before he starts on his mission, and his commander knows it, too. The only reason for the order being given is enemy obstruction and the need to overcome it if the battle is to be won.

Exactly the same principle is true in spiritual warfare, yet a lot of Christian soldiers seem to be saying to their Commander, "We can't advance because the enemy disapproves of our objectives and is not willing to let us pass."

Isn't that ridiculous talk? Of course he
disapproves; that's what makes him an enemy. Of
course he fights against the Lord's army; that's what
he must do if he is to stay in charge of things. Why,
then, are so many Christians amazed, and even
immobilized, at the least sign of resistance to the
gospel? Why are their feelings hurt when a sinner
scoffs at their witness? Why do they adjust their
programs for advancing the cause of Christ to
conform to the regulations and restrictions of
the enemy?

The simple explanation is that they are
forgetting their orders and who issued them.

The lordship of Christ

The very first principle for any Christian work is
this: the Lord Jesus Christ, who crushed Satan and
conquered death, commands us to invade this
enemy-occupied world and reclaim it for God. We
march under his exclusive authority and are
forbidden to make any deals with the foe. No
compromises. No concessions. And no excuses!

What's more, he has given his word that hell's
own gates ultimately will not hold out against the
advance of his church. All of the devil's maneuvers
and power-plays are just his last-ditch resistance to
the overwhelming force of the Righteous One. And

yet, thousands of Christians today are practically cowering in the face of hostile opposition to the gospel. If they still regard faith as a weapon at all, they seem to have placed it in their antique collection. The glorious promises of Jesus are regarded by far too many professing believers as little more than pretty mottoes.

Maybe our preaching has been at fault. The claims of the Kingdom of God ought to come first in our preaching, but we have diverted too much of that. We have overemphasized salvation in our evangelistic services and have neglected to present the claims of Christ upon the people. I think that is why we have made so many weak converts. We've made the forgiveness of sins and a clean heart the issue. It is not. The issue is the claims of Christ upon mankind.

In all our preaching we emphasize that a person is saved the moment Jesus has cleansed his heart from sins. Is that correct? In the Old Testament pattern of the Kingdom of God represented by the Tabernacle, a person is saved when he has entered through the door. Jesus said, "I am the door . . . if any man enter by me!" And once you've gone through the door, then the first thing you hit is the cross. Bunyan set exactly the same pattern in *Pilgrim's Progress*. You first enter through the gate, acknowledging the claims of Christ for your life. You first bow your knees—because he is King!

Very often in the experience of evangelists, conviction of sin comes after prayer. It's unfair to require conviction of sin before you will pray with a person. I think the strongest conversion is when a person says to you, "I don't want to serve the devil any more." Then you can lead him on to the cross for forgiveness of sin, and for cleansing and fellowship, and for communion with God himself. All of these are steps, but it begins when we acknowledge the rightful claims of Christ upon our lives. This is what the apostles preached.

"Him hath God exalted with his right hand to be a Prince and a Saviour" (Acts 5:31). God has not made Jesus a ruler and a judge, but a ruler and a redeemer—a Prince and a Savior—"for to give repentance to Israel, and forgiveness of sins." Here Peter is preaching the lordship of Christ. He doesn't say that God has made him a Savior and Ruler; he has made him Ruler and Savior, in that order.

The children of Israel had a similar confusion about Moses. According to Acts 7:35, they refused him, saying, "Who made thee a ruler and a judge?" God never made him a ruler and judge. God made him a ruler and a redeemer—a deliverer, not a judge. That's what the people thought, but they were wrong.

You will find those four words opposed in that one verse: the people said: "ruler and judge," but God sent him to be "a ruler and a deliverer."

Jesus is King! That's the starting point for conversion, and that's the starting point for Christian service. It is also the heart of the issue in our spiritual warfare, as the enemies of the gospel have known from New Testament days until now.

Who turns what upside down?

When Paul and his evangelistic group came to Thessalonica, the city council got scared at the report: "These that have turned the world upside down are come hither also" (Acts 17:6).

That's a lie, by the way. They had not turned the world upside down. Whenever a statement is made in the Scriptures, you must first find out who says it. This charge was made by the enemies of Christ, therefore it is a lie. Turn it around and you get to the truth.

It was the devil who turned the world upside down, and these men came to give it another turn to put it straight again! And such men are, of course, objected to by the governments of this world, who are all in the service of the evil one because this world is in the grip of the evil one.

Now this is a well-known verse, and I love it! I

wish every city council would get together the moment they hear about an evangelistic campaign by any Christian group, and I wish they would all get scared and say, "They turn the world upside down." It's about time we do!

But how did they do it? The sequel to this verse is in the next: they were saying that there is another king—Jesus! That is the issue. That's why they were afraid—not because they thought the Christians would start one or two more churches, but because they were preaching another *king*—Jesus!

This is the very reason that this message of the Kingdom of God is so hated by the Communists today. This is why in the Christian song books in the Soviet Union there are very few hymns on Christian warfare, or on the Second Coming. In a recent issue in East Germany where they wanted to reprint a hymn book, they had to take out all the hymns like "The Lamb upon the Throne" and "Onward, Christian Soldiers." It's a message of the other King. It's the message of the Kingdom. It's entering into the spiritual conflict, and that is the point where they are scared. That, then, is where we must stand.

The biggest statement ever made
When this glorious King commands us, it is not for us to question, or argue, or hesitate, or decide for

ourselves whether we will obey, and to what extent. That's complete foolishness. In fact, we should count it the highest privilege to leap into action at his slightest bidding, without a moment's thought for our own convenience or comfort.

Now, what are his orders to us?

"And Jesus came and said to them"—to his young followers, the disciples, relatives, friends— "All authority in heaven and on earth has been given to me. Go therefore and make disciples of all nations, baptizing them in the name of the Father and of the Son and of the Holy Spirit, teaching them to observe all that I have commanded you: and lo, I am with you always, to the close of the age" (Matthew 28:18-20).

One of the great battles which Jesus had faced for those last three years in training and educating his disciples was the fact that this message of God and the love of God for people was not confined to a small group, the Jewish nation, but indeed was for the whole world. How could he break through that barrier to make them think bigger than their own nation, or their own particular religion, as they saw it at that time?

Just a few weeks before he made this tremendous statement about his authority, Jesus had died on the cross. The Scripture tells us that he took

the sin of the *whole* world upon himself in his body
—not just the sin of the Jewish nation, not the sin of
tired religious people, but the sin of every atheist,
Communist, individualist, Buddhist, Muslim—the sin
of everyone who lived at that time and would ever
live in the future. This was a universal thing that
Jesus did! He took upon himself the sin of the
whole world.

Here he is facing the disciples for the last time
on the day of his ascension—the day on which he is
going to take his rightful place on the throne of God.
He has something tremendous to say to them, the
biggest statement that was ever made in this world.
He is going to send them into enemy territory. He is
seeing, as no one else possibly could at that time,
that the devil was the prince of this world, that the
devil would do everything he could to stop Jesus'
followers from spreading the message of what Jesus
had just accomplished on the cross for everyone. He
was going to reclaim men from the grip of Satan. This
was a battle cry, and Jesus was the only one who
knew *what* a battle! That's why he made that
tremendous statement: "*All* authority in heaven and
on earth has been given to me. It is placed in my
pierced hands."

I can just feel the impact of his words, for this
had never been said before. He was telling his little

group of followers that they were to go under his absolute authority into all the world to make disciples among all nations. This was not the wishful thinking of a dreamer. This was the explicit command of the all-knowing and all-powerful Son of God. He wasn't asking them, he was telling them!

Religion—the opiate of the people
Now, everyone could agree with the first part of the statement, that Jesus indeed has all authority in *heaven*. We don't dispute that, and that is probably the reason why we want to go to heaven. No war, no revolution, no sin, no sickness, no hatred; there is God, there is love, joy, peace, righteousness—that is the Kingdom of God. Possibly we just overemphasize all those things in heaven which we so easily believe because there is no way of checking up on it today. We can completely avoid the conflict of living as a Christian in this world by focusing our thoughts, our desires, and singing our hymns, all about heaven.

That is exactly why Karl Marx, who came from a Jewish Christian home (his family was converted to Protestantism when he was eight years old), took his pen and wrote a terrible rebuke to the Christian world: that religion is the opiate of the people.

Marx saw Christians dodging Christ's commands by failing to realize that he had not only said,

"All authority *in heaven* has been given me . . ."
but also "all authority *on earth*. . . ." By his "Go
therefore . . ." Jesus is opening the battlefield for us.
He is showing that this is a spiritual conflict, and that
he is now sending his disciples, or his followers (you
and me) into this enemy territory to claim people who
are held by the power of Satan in any form of sin,
behind any possible barrier—be it a cultural barrier,
a language barrier, or even a denominational or
political barrier.

That's the thing that concerns me so much
today. We have to make this very clear, that here is
the conflict that cannot be reconciled; it can only be
conquered by going and doing what Jesus told us.

When he tells us we must go and make
disciples of all nations, the assumption is that those
nations are not disciples. Here is a very interesting
thought from Watchman Nee, a great Chinese saint
who died recently after spending more than twenty
years in his Chinese prison. This is taken from his
devotional book *A Table in the Wilderness*. It's dated
January 10, and is a little commentary on Psalm 2:1,
"Why do the nations rage?"

> The answer is supplied at once: it is because
> the rulers take council together against the Lord
> and against his anointed. However violent the
> hostility between them, world governments are

at heart united on the wrong thing—they are
against the reign of Christ. We look upon the
nations as some of them bad, some good. E .t
Scripture points us to the Prince of this world
behind them all. Prompted by him, earth's
rulers today seek only absolute freedom from
sanctions imposed by the law of Christ. They
want no more love, no more humility, no more
truth. Let us break their bands asunder, they
cry, and cast away the cords from us. At this
point alone in all Scripture is God said to laugh.
His king is already on his holy hill. The early
church was very much aware of Christ's
dominion. More than ever today do we need to
remember it. Soon, maybe in our lifetime, he
will shepherd nations with a rod of iron. Our
task is to plead with men to be wise, to put their
trust in him.

The early church
He puts that beautifully. The early church was
aware of the conflict, realizing as one body that they
were set apart for a purpose: to conquer the world for
Christ, to make disciples of all nations.

Recognizing that Jesus sent them into enemy
territory, they also knew that they didn't need
anybody's permission. They were facing an enemy

not a human enemy, but inimical ideas, religions, or political philosophies that govern people, govern whole nations, and, indeed, today govern whole continents. That's the enemy they were facing. They did not need anybody's *permission;* they had only to obey the *commission!*

When Jesus ordered his disciples 2,000 years ago to move out with the gospel into all the world, there were just as many "curtains" obstructing their way as there are today—religious, political, cultural curtains—and yet they had to go, bringing the Word of God to people in bondage everywhere. Against deathly opposition, they invaded every corner of the Roman Empire.

The hearts of all men everywhere
I find great comfort for myself when I see that Jesus did not send us only to countries that would welcome us. That would be rather ridiculous. Yet we have thought that way entirely too long. In effect, we have sent missionaries largely to countries that put out the red carpet for us. Too long have we thought of "open doors" only in terms of a welcome to Christian workers.

But, for the Lord himself, are there ever any *closed* doors?

That question, of course, confronts us squarely

with the controversial subject of Bible-smuggling.
You see, I don't believe that our Lord is willing for
his Word and witness to be kept out of any country
by guarded boundaries or government decrees. That
would be contrary to both the spirit and the letter of
his commission to us to make disciples of all nations.
In fact, doesn't it make better sense to concentrate
efforts on those very spots that are most resistant to
the gospel, most dominated by the devil's power?

Sometimes when people try to argue with me
about this, I ask them what they think of the work of
TransWorld Radio, and Far Eastern Broadcasting
Company, and other radio stations that beam the
gospel into Communist countries. They say they are
all in favor of that. What is the difference? The
Russian government is just as much against the
gospel's being broadcast through the air as they are
against its being carried in a car or taken in person.
It's all the same thing to them.

Yes, it is the same resistance on their side, and
the same commission on our side. No difference—
except that there is less personal risk involved if you
get hold of a microphone and sit in Monte Carlo or
Manila while you broadcast. In principle it is the
same thing. Both means are effective; both have to
be done. For both we need dedicated young people.
But the invasion by the gospel is illegal as far as the

Communist government is concerned, and it is a very dangerous thing for us, I think, to apply a double standard of morals to equally vital Christian efforts.

Later I shall say more about these hostile governments. Right now, I simply repeat that the command of our King is to capture for him the hearts of all men everywhere who are in bondage to Satan.

A matter of obedience

Dr. Dotsenko, that brilliant nuclear physicist from Russia who defected to Canada some years ago, was asked what can be done for Christians in the Soviet Union and what he thought of smuggling Bibles into Communist countries. As reported in *Christianity Today*, he made this somewhat startling answer: "Do everything that your conscience, your courage, and your trust in God allow you to do. Shall we submit ourselves to this godless force? Or shall we follow the commandment of our Lord, 'Feed my sheep'?"

Then he made a rather flattering statement about our work: "I must confess that I admire Brother Andrew and his co-workers. I pray for them that the Lord will continue to keep them under his protection and inspire them for their further service. This is the true spiritual battle," he says, "where people risk their lives and personal freedom for their brethren to bring them the Word of God."

I am grateful for those words and for many
other insights of this man that have been helpful to
me personally. But I think his key statement, "Do
everything that your conscience, your courage, and
your trust in God allow you to do," is not quite
strong enough.

That makes the future of the whole world and
the coming of the Kingdom of God dependent on our
conscience, our courage, and our trust in God,
instead of on the commandment of Jesus Christ, "Go
into the world, . . ." which we must do regardless of
the actions of governments.

With all due respect to our brother, it's not a
matter of conscience, courage, and trust in God. It's
a matter of obedience. Here we come to that sensitive
point about relating to the government. Of course, we
must obey our government, but that goes only so far.
We must obey *unless* that government—whether it is
our own or the government of those nations where
God sends us as missionaries, as soul-winners, as
apostles, as evangelists, pastors, or smugglers—
unless that government takes the place of God.

You ask: Where can a government take the
place of God? In two realms: the realm of conscience
—in the service of Christ, in witnessing; the realm of
worship—because that's where they come with
persecution. God demands body, soul, and spirit—

this is very clear in the Scriptures. We have
compromised so badly with the world's systems,
though the Bible told us not to do it, that we hardly
know where any given government is in conflict
with God.

In no-man's land
Jesus told a little story to people who had a very
tricky question for him about paying taxes. He said,
in Matthew 22:20, after they had shown him a coin,
"Whose likeness and inscription is this?" And they
said, "Caesar's." Then he told them to render to
Caesar the things that are Caesar's, and to God the
things that are God's. When they heard that, they
marveled and left him and went away, unable to
make up their minds, and unwilling to make
a choice.

Our problem today is that there are millions of
Christians who cannot make up their minds, who
want to live in no-man's land, and get a little bit of
the left and a little bit of the right. Yet, at the end,
when they die, they want to go to heaven! They
never make a clear stand for Jesus Christ.

What Jesus is saying here is this: "This coin
indeed has the image of Caesar imprinted on it.
Now, if it has Caesar's imprint, give it to Caesar. But
if it has God's imprint, give it to God."

When he looks at the people, what does he
see? He sees people made *in the likeness of God*,
and he implies this: Give *that* to God, give *yourself* to
God! And I tell you that if you give yourself fully to
God, wholly, completely—there's nothing left for
Caesar. That is what Jesus is saying here.

If we would really come to the point where God
wants us—and he makes it so clear in Romans 12:1
("I appeal to you therefore, brethren, by the mercies
of God, to present your bodies, your person, as a
living sacrifice, holy and acceptable to God, which
is your spiritual worship. Do not be conformed to this
world, to this present system, the economy of this
world. Don't! Don't go in for that. Go in for the
Kingdom of God. Be a radical, or even a fanatic")—
then I would say it's easier to cool down a fanatic
than to warm up a corpse any day!

Basic unwillingness

Why are we not all out for Jesus Christ? Then we can
obey God, and we can obey all the governments
where their laws are in harmony with God's
expressed will. We know what God's will is. We just
try to dodge his commandments. That gets us into all
kinds of trouble. As William Penn said in 1681: "If we
are not governed by God, then we will be ruled by
tyrants." That is a very good remark.

Many people even try to substitute prayer for obedience. I have a great friend in one of the Communist countries; he is a well-known evangelist, a real scholar, but he doesn't work in his own profession—he works full time for the Lord Jesus. Once he said to me: "Brother Andrew, all those people who, when they want to work for the Lord, always ask permission where they think they should have it—whether from government, or a city council, or the police if they want to give out tracts, or have a campaign or an open-air meeting, or anything like that—indicate their basic unwillingness to get on with the job! If they were simply obedient, if they wanted to do it, they would do it . . . Jesus told them to do it. People wouldn't like it, or the governments would disagree. Well! They may get arrested, they may get into trouble, they may be called in for questioning. However, they can always explain, and they can always still apologize. But they must first do it."

I think he has a tremendous truth there. It's so plain, and still we don't realize that the governments of this world simply are not for Christ.

The Apostle Peter found this out very quickly, as we see in Acts 5. Right there in the beginning of the Church's life, of the ministry in public, the government disagrees with their message and their methods—apart from the fact that they disagree with the men. So they got arrested by their legal government, to which the Bible says you must submit yourself.

The main issue

In Acts 5:28, the high priest says: "We expressly ordered you to desist from teaching and preaching in that name, and what has happened? You have filled Jerusalem with your teaching and you are trying to make us responsible for that man's death."

Now listen to the reply Peter gave for himself and the apostles: "We must obey God rather than men."

That's it. Here again is the main issue: Jesus said we *must* take the gospel into every country. If any of those countries resist—whether the police, the government, the army, the culture, or even the religion—we still have the commission to go, regardless!

Seeing that the conflict is spiritual, we realize that only from the Bible can we find the answer as to what we should do today, what our actions and our attitudes ought to be toward governments. That includes our own government. Can we criticize our own government where we feel that it goes against God? Can we criticize other governments that are godless, cruel, persecuting the church? Is there any action that we can take in this respect if we know that there still are Christians who are faithful, who want to live under Christ's dominion? Is there any way we can help?

All those issues are just one: It's not a matter of ethics of smuggling; it's a matter of finding out who is in charge and who has the right to this world.

Here's an illustration from the Old Testament. In Daniel 3:5 we have the situation where King Nebuchadnezzar has set up a huge image and has called together all his people, including many Jewish prisoners who live there in exile, some of them having risen to high positions. This is the edict:

"When you hear the sound of the horn, pipe [and other musical instruments] you are to fall down and worship the golden image that King Nebuchadnezzar has set up; and whoever does not fall down and worship shall immediately be cast into a burning fiery furnace."

Now here was the government, the legal authority. It was acknowledged not just by the Babylonians but also by the Jews who had submitted themselves to it—including a man of God like Daniel. (I think he is the only one whose Bible biography records nothing negative against him.)

This great man of God had served as a

minister in three foreign governments. Therefore, he
surely acknowledged this as his legal government.
Yet his three friends, when they heard this decree,
and when the music was played and everybody fell
down before the image and worshiped, did not bow.
They refused. And they were cast into the fiery
furnace.

The government here was trying to take the
place of God. Remember that. But the amazing thing
is that when the authorities looked into the furnace,
they saw four men, not the three, walking free in the
midst of the fire, unharmed; and the appearance of
the fourth was like a son of the gods (Daniel 3:25).

What had happened? God had identified
himself with those who disobeyed the king's
command, because there was a more important issue
at stake, bigger than just the national issue—a
spiritual issue. Those who refused to obey the
ungodly decree were in the will of God and
preserved by him!

Justified by works

Another beautiful illustration is the story of Rahab.
In Hebrews 11:31, we read: "By faith Rahab the
harlot did not perish with those who were
disobedient, because she had given friendly
welcome to the spies."

Her action was a very illegal thing, because her local legal government was against Israel, and Israel was going to conquer her nation. Therefore, Rahab's duty was to her own king, her own government, her own people. Or was it? No, she had seen something else: she had seen the spiritual conflict (Joshua 2), and had chosen in her heart to follow the God of Israel, if only she could find out something about him.

The whole fascinating story unfolds when the soldiers (let's call them police) come to her home and say, "You have entertained men of Israel who have come here to search out the land. Take them out of your home. We are going to arrest them. Here is the arrest warrant. Our legal government wants them."

But the woman has taken the two men and hidden them. Listen carefully now to what she says. "True, men came to me, but I did not know where they came from." Was that the truth? No, it was not. "And when the gate was to be closed, at dark, the men went out." Was that the truth? No, it was not. "Where the men went I do not know." Was that the truth? No, it was not. "Pursue them quickly, for you will overtake them."

But she had brought them up to the roof where she hid them with the stalks of flax which she had laid out in order upon the roof (verse 6). This is what she did when those soldiers went to search outside the gate: she took the spies out quickly and let them out over the wall, and they escaped. First, though, she got their promise (verse 14) to spare her life and deal kindly with her when the Lord gave them her land.

That's an amazing story. She tells lies, she hides spies, she helps them escape, she does everything against her own legal government because behind it she sees another kingdom—the Kingdom of God—and she's going to risk everything in order to help the Kingdom of God, including telling lies.

Now, I don't condone telling lies, As far as my own ministry is concerned, I will never tell a lie. I determined that many years ago. But when I have a load of Scriptures and I go to a Communist country, determined not to tell a lie, I pray mighty hard that I don't have to tell the truth either, and this way we manage!

What about Rahab, though? Well, we may argue that she was a heathen woman, so she told lies. We may never tell a lie, but I still have to see the day when our names are written by God in Hebrews 11. Rahab is in! "By faith, Rahab the harlot did not perish with those who were disobedient, because she had given friendly welcome to the spies."

The Lord doesn't praise her for telling lies, but for her attitude—and not just her attitude, but indeed for her action as well. Look at James 2:25: "Was not also Rahab the harlot justified by works?" It's what she did, which was determined by what she believed. Action was a result of her attitude, her disposition, her allegiance. Now there was some heathen woman, all right!

Ethical concealment

Again in the Old Testament we find out about one of the greatest men of God, the great prophet Samuel. He had anointed Saul to be king, and then Saul proved unworthy of this great honor and God rejected him. Samuel was very sad about it. Then, in 1 Samuel 16:1, the Lord said to him: "How long will you grieve over Saul, seeing I have rejected him from being king over Israel? Fill your horn with oil, and go; I will send you to Jesse the Bethlehemite, for I have provided for myself a king among his sons."

Here is a very clear command which God gives in order to preserve Israel as a nation, not as his main purpose, but in order to maintain the line from which his Son, the Messiah, would be born. From the beginning of the Old Testament right up to the New, God worked hard to preserve that one line, in good times and evil times, whether occupied by the enemy or taken into exile, through times of apostasy or times of prosperity. God worked hard on that; and here he has made up his mind he is going to anoint David, a man after his heart, one of the people in the line of the Messiah.

But Samuel is afraid (verse 2). "How can I do that? If Saul hears it" (they were already living in a police state, a dictatorship) "he will kill me." They had gone that far. The devil was using a man who was anointed by the servant of God as the potential destroyer of the seed of Messiah; to kill so as to prevent the birth of Jesus Christ in Bethlehem thus making it impossible for the Kingdom of God to break through in this world. You may want to study that thought for yourself; God's work of preservation is written through the whole Scripture.

Whether it is the destruction of Joseph, or of the Israelites in Egypt, or anything else that happens in the Old Testament, it's all aimed by the devil to avoid the possibility of Jesus being born in Bethlehem —every detail, this one included.

"If Saul hears it, he will kill me." Samuel is afraid.

The Lord then said to Samuel, "Take a heifer with you."

Now wait a minute! Is God telling Samuel that he is going to hide his real errand? Cover it up? Do something that many people wouldn't even call ethical? Here the Almighty God himself instructs Samuel to cover up his action, to camouflage it and tell only part of the truth! I call this concealment of truth.

God says: "Now, listen, Samuel, this is what you do: you take a heifer with you, and if Saul's police stop you, you just smile at them and say, 'Oh, I'm going to sacrifice to the Lord; just look at this heifer. I am going to Bethlehem and I am going to invite Jesse to the sacrifice.'"

God said, "Samuel, while you do that, I will show you what more you shall do: you shall anoint for me him whom I name to you."

Well, this is God's divine authorization for concealment (hiding, let me call it) by means of a statement other than that which would have disclosed the main purpose of Samuel's visit to Jesse. You may call it evasion, or a suppression of the whole truth. But the most important fact is that there was no untruth in what the Lord authorized. The Lord will never do that. The issue here is this: Saul had no right to know the whole purpose of Samuel's mission to Jesse, nor was Samuel under obligation to disclose it. Concealment is not lying. You must be careful to guard the distinction between partial truth and untruth.

A matter of priority

As I have said before, I pray hard that I don't have to tell the truth. But it's not telling a lie, if I hide the truth from people who have utterly forfeited the right to know the truth.

If I stand at the Communist border and have my car loaded with Scriptures, then I am under no obligation whatsoever to tell them the truth, because they are in the service of the devil. Their aim is to prevent the Kingdom of God from coming to this world. And they do it with the most cruel means: suppression of the truth, killing off pastors and believers, imprisoning of millions of believers, burning down the churches. And these people, the guards and police, are all in that system: and though I love them as people, I surely don't love their system, because they are in the service of the devil himself, dedicated to stamp out the church so that the Kingdom of God will not come here in this world.

You see, here we have again the spiritual conflict. What is behind it? Why is King Saul going to be angry if he hears about Samuel's mission to Jesse—the anointing of David? The issue is another king instead of Saul!

Remember what we are saying: Jesus is the King of kings, and his orders take priority over all the decrees of human governments, especially when godless men try to restrict or prohibit the spread of the gospel and the pressing of Christ's claims upon the hearts of people. This is a fact of divine revelation which is not open to argument or rationalization. "We must obey God rather than men." It's that simple.

I have had many discussions on this with some very righteous people, whose sincerity I don't doubt for a moment, who think that smuggling Bibles is unethical. They say that if a government forbids the import of Bibles, then we should obey that particular government, whether it be Russian or Cuban or Chinese. Well, if you'd reason along that line it means that the apostles never would have come into any country in Europe. If you study the New Testament, you will see that there was not a single country that ever invited the apostles to come, nor even allowed them for that matter. On the contrary, they were persecuted. It was by going into hiding, or doing illegal things as far as the governments were concerned, that they succeeded in getting the gospel into Europe.

We remain under the same imperative today. We *must* get the gospel across to every creature. Whether we send in diplomats, businessmen, reporters, missionaries, evangelists, or smugglers, they all have just one purpose: to make Jesus Christ known in those nations by every possible means. We have no right to deny any person a chance to come to the knowledge of Jesus Christ our Savior. No government has the right to restrict any of the believers, whether in the West or in the Communist countries, from traveling and making God's Word known—spoken or written.

I repeat: no government has a right to restrict Christian believers from making Christ known, and that is the issue today. Are we going to obey God or men?

That kind of talk can only get you into trouble, some will say. Absolutely correct! A great Communist sports hero, Emil Zatupek, while visiting Indonesia as a kind of unofficial ambassador of his government, was led to Christ by a Swiss missionary there. Some time later, the missionary visited Zatupek in Czechoslovakia, and found that this one-time colonel was now a streetsweeper because of his stand for Christ. When I asked how Zatupek was doing, he said: "He is still following the Lord Jesus!"

"As though in prison with her"

In 1967, Maria Braun, a fine Baptist believer, was sentenced to five years' imprisonment in a labor colony. We printed that in our prayer letter, asking people to pray for her. On March 23, 1971, *Isvestia* published an article quoting a letter in which Maria denied her faith. She said that she had been justly sentenced because she had broken the law by teaching children about Christ.

I am not accusing Maria Braun. If she denounced Christ, I think I know the reason: not enough people were praying for her, not enough people were going in (as Hebrews 13 says) "as though in prison with her." Pastor Richard Wurmbrand of Romania, who spent 14 years in a Communist prison, titled a book: *If That Were Christ, Would You Give Him Your Blanket?*

If you had been in prison with Maria Braun, would you have given her your blanket? Would you have given her your bread? Would you have given her your Bible so that she could have strengthened herself in the Lord? Would you have given her your time, your love, your prayer, so that she would have been able to withstand terrible pressure, which she obviously was not able to stand?

This is a difficult point here: people supposedly giving up their faith in God because they cannot take the unbearable pressures any more. Only God knows where they really stand. That is why we ask people to pray, not just for us, but also for the persecuted church.

Maria Braun was charged with breaking the law. Many people say to me, "You are breaking the

law, because you are doing what you are not
supposed to do. If the law in a certain country says
that no Bibles are permitted, you should not bring
them in."

Now, what is the law? There are two laws, and
the first is the Law of God. When Jesus was asked to
identify the greatest commandment, he quoted verses
which every Jewish child knew from Deuteronomy 6:
"The Lord our God is one Lord; and you shall love
the Lord your God with all your heart, and with all
your soul, and with all your might. And these words
which I command you this day shall be upon your
heart . . . And you shall write them on the doorposts
of your house and on your gates . . . and you shall
teach them diligently to your children, and shall talk
with them when you sit in your house, and when
you walk by the way, and when you lie down, and
when you rise."

"You shall teach them to your children . . ."
That's God's law. Jesus reflected its spirit when he
said: "Let little children come to me."

Did Maria Braun break *that* law?

Now, here is another law of a godless regime
that says, "You cannot teach children about Jesus.
You cannot teach them to pray, teach them the Bible,
or take them to church. And they cannot be baptized;
it's forbidden."

There is the basic issue again: which law do Christians obey? Whose orders do they take?

Being nice to the devil

I want to be very plain here: if we are consistent in keeping the law of God, of necessity we will have to break the law of many governments. At this moment, in all the godless, atheistic governments where they tell us not to teach, not to take Bibles, we've got to break *that* law or break God's law.

If we do not reach all nations with the gospel—if we don't make disciples of all nations including Russia, Mongolia, Red China, Tibet (you can name all of the Communist countries)—if we write off any of them because we say that they are behind political borders and it wouldn't help our diplomatic efforts, but might even revive the Cold War, not to speak about the Hot War!—if we would go in and arouse anger and do things we are not "supposed" to do—well, all right: we are establishing for ourselves a tradition. *We want to be nice to the devil!* We even want to lend him a hand as he kills God's children and tries to prevent the coming of the Kingdom of God. In doing that, we definitely break the law of God!

That is the issue. We've got to see it. When they were threatened there in Jerusalem (Acts 5:27-29) and told not to teach or preach any more in the name of Jesus, Peter just turned his back to them and said: "We must obey God rather than men."

Here is the point: if we break God's commandment in order to stick to men's traditions, we let the devil continue to rule the world, and let Communism and atheism, and revolution, and hatred just sweep over the world. And violence, crime, war, and bloodshed will exterminate the church completely.

Or, we break with our lazy traditions and we start keeping God's commandment. He said: "Go into *all* the world, and make disciples of *all* nations." He also said: "Remember those who are in prison, as though in prison with them" (Hebrews 13:3).

A protest march?

Because the early church realized what the real problem and the real issues were in this spiritual conflict, they reacted in the right way when the apostles were flogged and then eventually released (Acts 4:23) and came to report what the chief priests and elders had said to them. What was that reaction when the church heard about the persecution?

"Let's take action! Let's bomb that nation! Let's fight them and kill them! Let's do something!"

No! That is *not* the way they reacted. When they heard the report, they lifted their voices together

to God (4:24). Instead of forming a protest march,
instead of writing to the United Nations, they held a
prayer meeting.

They said: "Sovereign Lord, who didst make the
heaven and the earth, and the sea and everything in
them, who by the mouth of our father David, thy
servant, didst say . . ." (and then comes a wonderful
prayer, and they acknowledged in verse 27) "for
truly in this city there were gathered together against
thy holy servant Jesus. . . ."

Jesus was in heaven, but he was still the issue.
They are fighting *Jesus*. They are not fighting our
system, not fighting capitalism or imperialism or
colonialism, not fighting western civilization—they
are fighting *Jesus*.

"And now, Lord, look upon their threats, and
grant to thy servants to speak thy word with all
boldness."

In other words, Lord, help us to step up our
efforts. We are not going to be intimidated. We are
not going to be scared because of the persecution and
the pressure, because it forces us to go underground.
We are not going to be pressed into hiding because
they persecute and kill us. Help us to be more bold
and stretch out your hand to heal. Signs and wonders
are performed "through the name of thy holy
servant Jesus."

This whole issue is still the same today, and that is what we have to see in our time. What so many regard as an ethical issue, saying, "Oh, you shouldn't smuggle; you should keep the law," is nothing but an agreement with the devil. In debating the morality of smuggling, we deny God the right to rule the world. And that's exactly why the devil rules it.

As we go back again to Matthew 28, we see that Jesus first claims that he has all authority, both in heaven and on earth, and then he commands, "Go therefore . . ." which implies that we do not need anybody's permission. We don't have to confer with our enemy, and have a nice conference or a cocktail party, to discuss our plans. No diplomacy here. We simply have to do it, because it is enemy-occupied territory and only one has the rightful claim to the world: that's God, through Jesus Christ, his Son! He redeemed men by his cross, and orders us to rescue them.

Sheer obedience, not conscience or courage, is our response!

The requirement of God's Word is submissiveness of heart to all authority, but absolute obedience only to God. In practical terms this means that Paul, Silas, Peter, and other disciples "(obeyed) God rather than men" and cheerfully accepted the consequences of prison sentences and death. They sang in prison, not in noisy protest, but in happy submission to authority and its consequences— "counting it all joy" to suffer for Christ's sake.

In 1 Samuel 19, King Saul commanded his submissive son, Jonathan, to kill David. Jonathan disobeyed the king and his father (though the Bible declares we should obey government and father) and even helped David to escape, yet God blessed Jonathan and the entire nation through his disobedience. Though we are submissive in attitude towards man's authority, our absolute obedience goes to the final and highest authority. "Thy will be done on earth, Lord Jesus."

A Look at the Warfare

On my last visit in Cuba, we had a conference on the grounds of the Church of the Nazarene near Havana. One evening, after a Methodist bishop spoke on the theme from Ephesians 6, "We wrestle not against flesh and blood, but against principalities," I had a talk with an Orthodox priest, a real born-again man.

"Andrew," this brother said to me, "I don't believe that with weapons we can do anything against Communism. It is a spiritual power. Three times a day when I go to prayer, I bind all the Communistic, atheistic powers in the air—and I battle in the heavens!"

"Praise the Lord, brother," I said. "This is the place to wrestle. You will accomplish something for the Kingdom of God, breaking down the stronghold of the devil."

What I want you to see now is the extremely important—no, that is putting it too mildly—the *only* requirement for being effective in carrying out the command of our Lord Jesus to invade enemy-occupied territory and reclaim it for God. It's just this: to do spiritual warfare, we must have an understanding of the *invisible world*.

Many Christians are confused about this, and the result is misunderstandings and mistakes. The real enemy of Christ is not some temporary political regime, however godless it may be. No, his adversary is the devil himself, as always, and our battle as believers in God is against the satanic forces that are running wild in the world.

Not by might or power . . .

The Word of God is very clear about the reality of the invisible world. In 2 Kings 2, Elijah, that great giant of God, is going to depart this life, and he knows it. It is a privilege for a servant of God to know so much about the future that until the last moment he can fulfill his ministry.

Walking with him that day is the younger man, Elisha. Do you remember the story? This is the way it begins:

> "And it came to pass, when the Lord would take up Elijah into heaven by a whirlwind, that Elijah went with Elisha from Gilgal. And Elijah said unto Elisha, Tarry here, I pray thee; for the Lord hath sent me to Bethel. And Elisha said unto him, As the Lord liveth, and as thy soul liveth, I will not leave thee." (2 Kings 2:1, 2)

Isn't that something? Elisha is so determined to find out God's best for his life that he will not settle for second best as too many people do. So they went together to Bethel. The students in the school of evangelism there say to Elisha, "Don't you know that the Lord will take away your master from you today?"

"I know it," Elisha says. "You just keep quiet." (That's my translation, by the way!)

Again, Elijah says: "Now you stay here, boy. The Lord has sent me to Jericho."

"No, I will stick with you," insists Elisha.

So they went to Jericho, where another bunch of evangelism students said the same thing to Elisha. And again Elijah told him to stay there because the Lord had sent him to Jordan.

"I will not leave you," Elisha said again.

At the Jordan, fifty Bible school students "stood afar off" while Elijah and Elisha stood by Jordan.

I tell you, there was a desperate situation in Israel. There were plenty of Bible schools, but very few men of God with the determination to press forward for full blessing.

Then (verse 8) Elijah took his mantle, rolled it up and struck the waters, which divided so the two men could go across just as the Israelites had passed through the Red Sea. On the other side, Elijah said: "Ask what I shall do for you."

What if Elisha had consented the first time that Elijah told him to stay behind? He would never have heard that question, "What shall I do for you?" You see what a man could miss by not sticking to to his purpose?

In reply, Elisha says: "I pray you, let a double

portion of your spirit be upon me." This is the way I interpret that:

"Elijah, you are a terrific man, even naturally —you are a giant in every sense of the word. I am just a poor farmer's son. I don't have that character, that personality, that you have. And you are undoubtedly the leader of Israel. There are plenty of Bible schools, but we don't see new leadership coming from there. It looks as though God is going to call me to leadership. How can I ever stand in your shoes unless I have twice as much Holy Spirit as you have to make up for my natural lack in comparison to you as a person?"

That is exactly what he is asking. It shows that he is a spiritual man. He knows that it is not by might or power, but by the Spirit of God, that ministry is performed.

Insight into the techniques of God
Incidentally, Elisha does not make the mistake that so many people do in missionary societies that have been founded by great men, thinking that they as missionaries can do the same as the founder. They *cannot!* That is in German *einmalig*. It is only once that God calls a man like Hudson Taylor or C. T. Studd. You cannot imitate a man who has been given special qualities from God to do a great

pioneer job or a great job in leadership. I repeat, you cannot imitate him!

There is a way, however: if . . . IF . . . only God would give you twice as much Holy Spirit as he has, then you could do the job, couldn't you? That is what Elisha had been thinking for a long time. That's why he didn't want to let go of his master. So now he expresses his strong, passionate desire that twice as much Spirit be upon him as there was upon Elijah.

Now we come to the point of this whole story, as the elder prophet makes his reply:

"You have asked a hard thing. Nevertheless, if (and that is a big *if*, an important *if*) you *see* the invisible world—if you have insight into the techniques of God—if you see me when I am taken from you, then it shall be unto you. If not, it shall not be so."

God is not going to waste the fullness of his Holy Spirit on a person who is too undecided and uncommitted to use it to the full.

Now, this is a principle of the importance of preparation. Don't think that you can just sit at home and skip all training, and discipline, and Bible school, and prayer, because you suppose that the fullness of the Holy Spirit is going to make up for all of that. You won't even *get* the blessing, not the first part of it. Elisha had been a faithful disciple of

Elijah for a long time before he came to this climax.
But now he realized as never before that the true
nature of the battle was spiritual, and could only be
fought out on a spiritual level.

If you and I can see that, then God will give us
all that we need to conquer the enemy and to
proclaim Christ and to reclaim his children. But we
bring to him all of our talent and all of our training,
to be put at his disposal, when we ask him for the
fullness of his Holy Spirit.

I wish I could have heard the conversation
between those two men! It must have been *highly*
spiritual. They knew that Elijah was going to
heaven any minute, but they didn't know how.

Then, suddenly, as they walked and talked,
behold! There appeared a chariot of fire and
horses of fire, and parted them both asunder, and
Elijah went up by a whirlwind into heaven, *and
Elisha saw it!* Glory to God! He saw it happen. He
saw heaven's taxi. He saw Elijah just shoot up into
heaven as the disciples later would see Jesus go
into heaven.

Elisha saw that which no one else could see:
he saw the *invisible world*. To him it was visible.
What a tremendous moment! I can well understand
his cry, "My father, my father: the chariot of Israel
and the horsemen thereof."

Then Elisha tore his own clothes into pieces because he did not need them any more, since he now had the mantle that had fallen from Elijah. He went back and stood by the bank of Jordan with that mantle of Elijah.

A terrific start for a ministry

Can you picture what happened next? On the other side of the river were still those fifty Bible school students who had seen a miracle when the two men went through earlier. Now Elisha is coming back alone, the Jordan is flowing as normal again, and what will happen?

With the mantle in his hand, Elisha calls out: "Where is the Lord God of Elijah?" He strikes the waters with the mantle, they separate as before, and he walks over.

What a tremendous story! It shows that the authority from the unseen world comes to a man through his insight, his contact, his fellowship with the unseen world—and is made manifest in the visible world!

That was a terrific start for Elisha's ministry. Could it have been just a fluke? Was it only the special circumstances, perhaps, that accounted for the special effects? Sometimes we wonder that about unusual manifestations. Well, we don't have to leave

the question unanswered where Elisha is concerned.
Look at 2 Kings 6, for instance.

Elisha and his servant are in the city of Dothan
that is besieged by a big enemy army, many
thousands. When the servant got up early in the
morning, he saw this huge host of horses and
chariots surrounding the city. "Alas, my master, how
shall we do?" he asked.

Surely there are many people today who can
sympathize with his despair as they look out on the
overwhelming forces that seem to be tightening the
net around their lives.

Listen to Elisha's answer: "Fear not: for they
that be with us are more than they that be with
them" (verse 16). Doesn't that sound a lot like 1 John
4:4: "He who is in you is greater than he that is in the
world." That is a statement of faith. Never forget it!

Then we read that Elisha prayed. Let me give
you my own translation of that prayer:

"Lord, I pray you, open his eyes that he may
see for a split second what I always see—day and
night."

God answered Elisha's prayer: he opened the
young man's eyes to see that the mountain was full
of horses and chariots of fire 'round about Elisha.
For just that moment, he saw the invisible world
because Elisha prayed. It was not his daily portion,

not his life, not his walk in the Lord; but for a
moment he saw what Elisha was always very much
aware of—the invisible world all around him:
angels, which according to Hebrews 1 are
ministering spirits sent out on behalf of those who
inherit eternal life.

This, then, has been the experience of those
men and women of God who were mightily used.

Press on to a full view

I think we really ought to include Moses in this
survey. After he studied for forty years all the great
sciences of Egypt, he spent the next forty studying
nothing but "sheepology"—no doubt also a lot of
"kneeology" more than theology. He led his flocks
to a remote part of the desert and came to Horeb,
the mountain of God. "And the Angel of the Lord
appeared unto him in a flame of fire out of the
midst of a bush: and he looked, and, behold, the
bush burned with fire, and the bush was not
consumed."

Here is Moses' first contact with the invisible
world—and it was about time: he was almost 80 by
now! He then received from God a commission
which he was deathly afraid to accept. He did all he
could to persuade God to give the commission to
someone else. Like many in the Christian church

today who say, "Lord, here am I; send my sister," so
Moses said, "Send my brother. Send Aaron." He did
all he could to get away from the call of God. It's
pathetic to see what had happened to that once
mighty man in forty years.

However, it would be doing Moses a real
injustice to pass lightly over that scene. The reference to it in Acts 7, beginning at verse 30, brings out
a very significant fact. When Moses saw the burning
bush and heard the voice speaking to him from it,
"he drew near to behold it." He was not afraid of the
invisible world; he did not run from the angel.

I think—this is a very private opinion now—
that most people are so extremely frightened of
angels that every time in the Bible when those
remarkable beings appear they commence their
message with the words "Fear not." Why is that?
Because people apparently have an extreme fear
when the invisible world breaks through into the
visible. Moses saw the angel and came close. Do
we have an appetite, a longing, for the invisible
world? Are we willing to press on to a full view?

A modern Sadducee

Let me turn now to a modern example. When I was
in Indonesia a few years ago, I got hold of a
biography of President Sukarno, written in English

by Cindy Adams. It was very interesting for me as a
Dutchman, because the Dutch have not always
treated him very kindly (he was a revolutionary all
his life, and the Dutch imprisoned him, deported him
to New Guinea, and what have you). When he saw
his chance, he took it, of course, and fought the
Dutch, who fought back. At one time, I was there
fighting him.

As I read Sukarno's biography, I understood a
lot of it. Here are some sentences from Chapter 33,
called "Reflections":

"Friends complain that my speeches lately are
peppered with references to the time when I
shall eventually leave them. Consciously or
unconsciously, I am readying them and myself
for a certain moment when every human being
will be called into the presence of the Almighty.
I believe strongly in the Hereafter. I also believe
that there are invisible angels near me at all
times. The angel at my right does the good
deeds. When comes the day of reckoning, he'll
brag: 'Here, Sukarno, are all of your good deeds.
Look at them.' Then the angel on the left will
gloat: 'Ah, Pak (that means "father"), but your
vices and dread sins, you will note, make a
much longer list; and that being the case, I am
afraid we have no choice but to send you to

hell.' I very much fear that if there is really a doorkeeper in the house of the Lord, and if he is going to have the say where I go, then alas, I shall probably plunge straight to hell. I don't dare hope where he will send me. I hope only that when my time comes, it will be over quickly."

I was deeply struck when I read this. I saw how a man who was hailed and almost worshipped when he was in power, and had been dropped by almost everyone when he was stripped of his power, here expresses his fear of death. I could have wept.

"Now there you are, Andrew," I thought to myself, "fighting against a man. You're just working on his going to hell. What are you doing for him?"

I prayed about it. I had one strong urge: a deep longing to see Sukarno and to pray with him. So I traveled to Djakarta, the capital city, and I went to the palace.

"Could I see the general?" I asked.

Strangely enough, they just let me in. The general who was in charge of all such things received me. "What can I do for you, sir?" he said.

"I want to see Sukarno."

"Why?"

"I have read his biography and have seen on

the last page that he is afraid to die. I want to speak
with him about Jesus. I want to pray with him so
that he can die and go to heaven."

The general, who was a Muslim, of course,
looked at me. Surely he had never heard that
before! Then he said to me a very strange word:

"I much appreciate your concern for Sukarno,
but this is not the time to think of the life of one
man. This is a time to think of the life of a whole
nation."

I thought I had heard that before! It's in John
11:50, where Caiaphas said it was better for one man
to die than for the whole nation to perish.

I pleaded with the general, but no matter what
I said, he would not let me in. They kept Sukarno
like a prisoner in one of his palaces. I was not
allowed even to talk about my desire, because then,
he threatened, the officials would have to throw me
out of the country.

"Well," I said, "I haven't talked to anybody,
except to my Lord."

At that, he just mellowed. As we had another
cup of coffee, I had opportunity for almost an hour
to preach the gospel to him. I thought: if I can't get
through to Sukarno, then *you'll* hear the gospel. As
I spoke about Jesus, it was remarkable how open
this man was.

"Later," he said to me, "after the elections, you may try again. You may apply for a visa from his nephew, the ambassador in Bonn, Germany. Then maybe we can let you."

Later, though, when I was abroad, I read in the papers that Sukarno had died. Undoubtedly he went to a Christless grave unless something or someone got to him, because he certainly knew the gospel.

A good friend of mine, a rear admiral of the Indonesian fleet and a very fine, Spirit-filled Christian, had often preached the gospel to Sukarno. On his big flagship of the Indonesian Marine Navy, he entertained many foreign guests, including heads of state from all the Communist countries. Whenever they were having a banquet, or any meal, he always insisted on saying a prayer *aloud*. Many people in Indonesia have heard the gospel through such a faithful witness as that. Who knows whether a believer was able to see Sukarno since he wrote that page?

The point is that Sukarno expressed his firm belief in the invisible world. Yet I am appalled at the lack of faith of many Christians in the invisible world. They are just like the Sadducees in the New Testament who did not believe in angels or in resurrection.

If, on the other hand, we *do* believe in the

invisible world, if we believe in angels, then no
borders are closed, no doors barred! The key to the
whole problem in the world today is that the
spiritual struggle is not Communism versus
capitalism, but the Prince of the power of the air, the
Prince of darkness, against the Lord Jesus Christ,
who is the Prince of Glory and the Savior of the
world! Unless we see that our real battle lies in the
realm of the invisible spiritual forces, we will never
have enough authority to *act* against *governments*—
and that's just exactly what God wants us to do!

Going back to Paul
Ah, now the objections begin to rise! How can any
law-abiding Christian advocate actions against the
government? What about the Scripture's teaching of
submission to those in authority over us? Why resist
the "powers that be" when they are "ordained
of God"?

    As we shall see shortly, this is an area of
woefully fuzzy thinking by masses of well-meaning
Christians, including some of the most prominent
churchmen in the world. To get at the heart of the
problem, we must examine carefully two things:
(1) What does the Bible truly teach about the
relationship between a Christian, who is a citizen of
the Kingdom of God, and the temporal authority of

his earthly government; and (2) What is the true nature of human systems of government?

The Apostle Paul's significant discussion of this whole matter in Romans 13 is especially interesting to me as a Dutchman with a Calvinistic background. In the Netherlands during the war when we had five years of German occupation, some fine believers, on the basis of Romans 13, cooperated with the German occupation army, considering it to be the legal government because Paul said there was no power or authority but what is instituted by God.

Let's give that passage the close look it deserves:

> Let every person be subject to the governing authorities. For there is no authority except from God, and those that exist have been instituted by God. Therefore he who resists the authorities resists what God has appointed, and those who resist will incur judgment. For rulers are not a terror to good conduct but bad. Would you have no fear of him who is in authority? Then do what is good, and you will receive his approval, for he is God's servant for your good. But if you do wrong, be afraid, for he does not bear the sword in vain; he is a servant of God to execute his wrath on the wrongdoer. Therefore one must be subject, not only to avoid God's wrath but also

> for the sake of conscience. For the same reason
> you also pay taxes.

Paul said that there is no authority except from God,
but he surely does define the kind of authority and
government that he has in mind. He said that they
protect the good, and he who does good will receive
their approval, because the ruler is God's servant
for the people's good.

Is that really the case with godless authorities?

Paul has another statement to make on this in
1 Timothy 2:1-4.

> First of all, then, I urge that supplications,
> prayers, intercessions, and thanksgivings be
> made for all men, for kings and all who are in
> high positions, that we may lead a quiet and
> peaceable life, godly and respectful in every
> way. This is good and it is acceptable in the
> sight of God our Savior, who desires all men
> to be saved and to come to the knowledge of
> the truth.

Again, along with his mention of the government,
the power that's put over us, he *defines it*. He said
the task is to protect the good. Writing to Timothy,
he makes it clear that the task is to insure that we
have religious liberty so that we can fulfill the laws
of Christ. What is *his* law? He desires that all men
be saved and come to the knowledge of the truth.

This idea he links to our prayer and our attitude toward a legal government.

In other words, if a government, local or national or international, limits the church in its activity, and curbs the witness of Christians and even persecutes them, then we are no longer under any obligation to observe this government in this respect of conscience and worship. We are free, because God has defined what the role of the government is. To obey government and to oppress the church would be just as silly as when the Dutch obeyed the German occupation army, or as it would have been for the Jews to obey Hitler. Some wrongfully did, through a wrong interpretation of Romans 13.

I am so glad that the Bible makes it clear. In the New English Bible, that verse in Timothy reads: ". . . that we may lead a tranquil and quiet life in full observance of religion. . . ." What is full observance? To go into all the world, in obedience to our Lord's command. Whenever any government restricts the traveling of the Christians to witness, then we must go directly against the government.

You ask if I have any scriptural proof for that? I'll just have to go back to Paul, because when anybody makes a statement, I think we should examine his life to see what he meant by those words. Your own life is the best interpretation of your doctrines and your statements.

In Acts 9:23, Paul was in Damascus where the Jews plotted to kill him. That was not an individual thing; it was the government. They had an official warrant of arrest. Paul was in for trouble, because instead of persecuting the church as the rulers in Jerusalem had commissioned him to do, he was now witnessing for Jesus Christ after his wonderful encounter with the risen Lord.

We read that "their plot became known to Saul. They were watching the gates day and night . . ." (Acts 9:24). Who was watching? The government. Police. Soldiers. Then his companions helped him get away at night by lowering him in a basket down over the wall.

Paul does a terribly illegal act there! He should submit to the government; haven't they the power of God?

No! Paul says. To observe fully the commandments of Christ, I must not let them limit my activities. Inasmuch as I've already received the commandment to go and do it, I am not going to be bogged down by any government decree. If they plan to arrest me, I'll just sneak out over the wall so I don't have to go through the border crossing to show my passport.

The apostle simply disregarded all the rules that other people who are not particularly in his business should observe. Did you ever wonder: "Paul, why were you so often in prison?" I think he would just whisper to you: "It was not for doing legal things, but always for doing illegal things."

Paul's overruling authority

Almost the same situation occurred in Iconium (Acts 14:6). The people were trying to molest him and stone him. He and his companions learned of it and fled to Lystra and Derbe where they preached the gospel.

They fled!

You shouldn't flee, Paul. You shouldn't run out. Why, you should submit to the government.

No! says Paul. Not when they restrict me in my witness for Jesus Christ. Then I must go against them and do what Jesus told me, and let no one interfere with me.

Again, (Acts 17:5, 6) he is in Thessalonica, where people want to attack the house of Jason, seeking to bring Paul's group out so that they can take him before the local legal government. But they couldn't find him. Why not? Paul had hidden. He had concealed his mission—he had gone under-ground, if you want to use that term. He was not going to show up and allow his witness and work to be destroyed by the enemy. He was not going to submit to what people would call his legal government.

The same situation arises again in Ephesus (Acts 19:30, 31). Paul wished to go in among the crowd, the mob that was trying to stir the city into confusion because Paul had made so many converts there. Secular historians tell us there were 20,000 converted people in one city! No wonder there were no sales for their goddess Artemis of the Ephesians!

Although that's remarkable, I want to say at this point that when they made a case of this, the government of the city admitted that in almost three years of preaching in Ephesus, Paul never said one word against the goddess. He said so much for Jesus that there were 20,000 converts anyway!

We have a positive message and a positive ministry. I believe in that. I don't want to run down any people who are negative; I don't really want to waste my time on it.

There in Ephesus, Paul has the nerve to go in among them to defend himself and to witness—but his companions would not let him. They hid him, they forced him to get out of the city, and they took the blame for whatever Paul did. This is a very important point. Paul knew what he was doing, and the Christian believers knew the real issue: they knew that the governments were against God, and therefore they had a more important business—they were under higher authority than the authority which the governments had.

At the end of Romans 14, Paul puts it this way: "The faith that you have, keep between yourself and God; happy is he who has no reason to judge himself for what he approves. But he who has doubts is condemned if he eats, because he does not act from faith; for whatever does not proceed from faith is sin." That's why it is so important for us to know where we stand in this issue of authority and obedience to governments.

It is perfectly clear from Paul's life that his pride in his Roman citizenship and his general loyalty to the laws of the Empire never took the place of his unreserved obedience to the Lord Jesus Christ, even when it meant conflict with Rome to the death! He respected authority, but he knew which authority had the supreme claim on his allegiance.

Peter as a V.I.P.

Not all of the New Testament teaching on governments comes from Paul, of course. Peter is another classic example of a colorful character in the early church whose statements and experiences are worth examining. Look at 1 Peter 2:13-17.

Be subject for the Lord's sake to every human
institution, whether it be to the emperor as
supreme, or to governors as sent by him to
punish those who do wrong, and to praise those
who do right. For it is God's will that by doing
right you should put to silence the ignorance of
foolish men. Live as free men, yet without using
your freedom as a pretext for evil; but live as
servants of God. Honor all men. Love the
brotherhood. Fear God. Honor the emperor.

He is saying that authority is to be honored, and that
God is to be feared. He says the governments must
comply with this criterion: they must punish the
wrong and praise those who do right. If this is not so,
then the whole structure falls apart and there is no
reason to obey such a government.

Well, Brother Andrew, you ask: how do you
prove that? Again, we just have to turn to the record
of the man who spoke those words. The famous case
is in Acts 5:17 and following.

Here Peter was in a situation where he was
under pressure by the government which he had to
honor and obey—the government that was supposed
to punish the bad and praise the good—and which
had put him in prison. While there, he was treated
like a V.I.P.—Very Important Prisoner—with sixteen
soldiers guarding him!

What happened? At night, an angel from the Lord opened the prison doors. Highly illegal! You can't just open the prison doors like that, because they were closed and sealed by order of the government that was put there by God. Correct? But what does *God* do? He identifies with the man who defied that government. God himself takes Peter out of prison.

What's more, God doesn't say to Peter: Now disappear, become an underground evangelist. No! He says: Go and stand in the Temple; speak to the people the words of life.

Doesn't that strike you as humorous, really? God is not afraid of a confrontation with the powers of evil. We are the ones who are scared because we don't know the real issues. That's why some are still debating the morality of so-called smuggling—which isn't smuggling at all: it's only obeying God rather than men!

Naturally, the authorities catch up with Peter again and say: "We strictly charged you not to teach in this name" (an official government decree) "yet here you have filled Jerusalem with your teaching and you intend to bring this man's blood upon us."

Then came Peter's wonderful response: *"We must obey God rather than men."*

There is a choice, you see. You can obey man,

sure! And the government, sure! You need not do anything for Jesus in your whole lifetime. You can obey men instead of God—and let the whole world go to hell!

A text out of context is a pretext
If we are going to cite the Bible as our authority, we dare not take single verses out of their total context. Submission to civil, legal authorities is a principle that the Scriptures very clearly and carefully qualify.

There is, of course, the closely related question: what is a "legal" government? If an occupation army comes, is that *your* government? Or are the authorities in exile, or underground, your legal government?

The same question pertains specifically to the matter of Communist dictatorship. None of the governments in eastern Europe are there by the choice of the people through free elections. I dare say that 95 percent of the population hates the governments in eastern Europe, including Soviet Russia. Is that even their *legal* government? You could doubt that.

At any rate, it surely is not *ours*. Nor is it a God-appointed government, inasmuch as those authorities act against the expressed will of God that the gospel shall be preached to everyone. They fight against that. Therefore, we just bypass them, and go our own way in the carrying out of the Great Commission of Jesus Christ the Lord.

That brings me to direct consideration of that second question which was posed earlier: What is the true nature of human systems of government? In principle, all earthly authority derives from God under his sovereign will. In practice, however, most earthly authority has sold out to Satan, and exists as the visible expression of his demonic force in the invisible world. God's angels are working in that invisible world on behalf of God's servants, but we must never forget that the fiends of hell are desperately active in the invisible world, too. In the plan of God, rulers are meant to be his agents for good; but in defiance of his plan, far too many of them are the devil's agents for wrong and evil and sin.

It is inevitable and unavoidable that we give primary attention to Communism in this regard. There are at least two reasons to do so.

First, when I talk about Communism, I do not talk about a political party, but about a religion. Communism is more a religion than any other so-called religion I know of; it's a religion of involvement, of extreme dedication, and as such, it is the most effective religion in the world.

Second, this is the first time in history when *one organization*—call it Communism if you want to, but it's not mainly a political issue—with the most cruel methods is trying to wipe out the entire church. To be sure, there has been opposition and persecution directed at the church before, but always on either a local or national level, never on a worldwide scale as now. More people may have died for their faith in Jesus in our generation than in the twenty centuries of Christianity put together. About half the world today, under the political cloak of Communism, is united in one big deliberate effort to annihilate Christ's church. And they are getting there—not slowly, but *fast!*

Obviously, both of those facts about Communism —that it is a religion and that it is dedicated to destroying the church—require me to explain more fully their bearing on the special work that the Lord has called me and my friends to do.

Dead men

The thing that got me going some seventeen years ago was hearing about a Communist youth móvement with 97 million members. By now the number in those young Communist leagues has swelled to 120 million members, making it by far the largest organization in the world. As faithful followers of their party line, they are being trained for world revolution and they are going to risk their lives to succeed.

Years ago when Khrushchev was still in power, he stood at Red Square in Moscow and spoke with very scriptural words to the massed troops of the Russian army: "You are all dead men!" He implied that in principle they had already lost their lives to the party. Then he added: "Now, go into the world and prove it!"

In effect, Christ said that to his disciples.

Yes, Communism is a religion; therefore, our battle with it is spiritual. I do not believe that any military action in the world, whoever undertakes it, will do *anything* to smash the power of Communism. On the contrary: since Communism is a religion, it has two elements that are essential to any religion: one, a common foe; two, a purpose for the future.

Communism must always have an enemy, or it cannot possibly exist. That is the basis of their religion. If they don't have an enemy, they make one, as Mao did when he started his cultural revolution. He had to do it to keep Communism going in China. He must create a foe if there is none.

Now, as far as China is concerned, either America or Russia is her Enemy No. 1. If Russia and China are reconciled, and if they make a deal with

America, then something else will happen because they *must* have an enemy. Inside the country or outside, they must always have this struggle in order to thrive. Call it capitalism, call it religion—the name makes little difference: they will keep on struggling.

It's frightening to see how far they will go, even creating an enemy within their own circles as Mao did. His friends, with whom he had fought side by side for fifty years, his fellow-ministers in Peking— he simply made them his enemies in order to keep his people behind him. It's fearful to watch that. We will never be able to have peace in the world as long as there is Communism.

Nor will we ever conquer Communism as long as we put our trust in men, because it is a spiritual power. It can be opposed and overcome only by another spiritual power. Which other spiritual power is available? The church of Christ!

Therefore, in those countries where the church of the Lord Jesus is being suppressed, persecuted, and almost wiped out, as in China, the official church at least in Albania, in North Korea, and Tibet —four Communist countries without any church— there we have to be especially under divine obligation to step in and do something that their governments strongly disagree with, that is highly illegal from their point of view. We have got to do it for the sake of Christ and for the sake of the whole world for which he died.

The worst enemy
That is our position in our mission. That's why I don't want to argue for long with people who say that smuggling is immoral. I don't want to waste my time. It's a great commission and command that we go in and preach Christ's deliverance to the captives; to win others to the Lord—yes, to win Communists for Christ! To do all of that requires, first of all, that we strengthen the brethren.

It *is* a spiritual battle. Therefore, we must become spiritual people, and must see the spiritual principles involved before we can be of any use, before we can effectively minister in this world.

Dr. Dotsenko very correctly observes that for Communists the ideological enemy is the worst enemy. Their hottest hatred, therefore, and their fiercest persecutions, are focused on Christian believers. The volume of documentation proving this is overwhelming, and constitutes a human scandal that has been brought to the attention of international councils time after time to no avail.

On February 1, 1972, the Norwegian Parliament (Storting) conducted a full debate on the persecution of Christians behind the Iron Curtain —

the first time that any national body had done such a thing. The official wording of the parliamentary question was: "Can anything be done on the part of Norway to end the persecution of Christians the other side of the Iron Curtain?"

During the speeches by leading members of Norway's political parties, the reliability and credibility of the reports of persecutions were never once questioned. Records were produced telling of imprisonment, children separated from parents, meetings disrupted, homes destroyed.

Karl Aasland, Storting Representative of the Centre Party, said: ". . . what appears to be clear enough is that some of these countries knowingly and systematically obstruct the freedom to practice one's religion, and it can hardly be open to doubt that this is part of a policy the purpose of which is a gradual mental breaking-down process, and the extermination of all religion. The most serious and dangerous aspect of all this is the complete denial of choice, and the atheistic ideology under which children and young people are forced to grow up."

He added: ". . . in my opinion, the central point here is the dissociation in principle from existing religion, not least the fact that Communist ideology cannot be reconciled with the Christian view of life."

Episcopal concern

The Norwegian Convocation of Bishops had earlier issued a strong statement on the matter of persecutions, in which they said in part:

> Officially there prevails in these countries full freedom of religion. One should, however, realize that Christian evangelization is being restricted to such an extent that believers are deprived of the basic opportunities to witness to their faith. Christians who violate such restrictions are being punished as enemies of the state and as offenders of civil law. In reality they are, however, punished for their faith. They are punished because they take their faith seriously and in accordance with the Master's words try to convert people. We would feel like traitors against the cause of the gospel itself if we forget this, if we fail to speak up against this, and if we neglect to do that which is within our power to build a world-wide opinion against this.

Now, frankly, I must confess that I am bewildered by some of my Christian friends who say, "Brother Andrew, you should stop what you are doing because it is illegal, or even immoral." I don't understand that. Here I learn that the Norwegian Parliament regards the documented persecutions of

Christians behind the Iron Curtain as crimes against humanity, and it appeals through their Foreign Minister to the United Nations Commission on Human Rights to act forcefully to curb such violations of the international charter.

Also, I hear the Bishops of Norway defending those persecuted Christians and summoning the whole world to protest against the outrages being perpetrated against them. They say the Christians are being punished officially for breaking the laws of their governments, but unofficially for their belief in Christ.

Yet, my critics tell *me* that I must not break those same inhuman and indecent laws of those Communist governments in order to help our brothers who are being persecuted for their faith and their faithfulness. Isn't that bewildering, indeed? Why should *I* obey laws which my fellow-Christians behind the Iron Curtain are breaking for their faith, and which the international tribunals denounce as illegal restrictions? It surely doesn't make sense to me!

Touchy matters

Let me illustrate this whole situation with direct reference to the matter of Bibles. Some agencies are claiming more and more that Bibles are available in

the Iron Curtain countries. The United Bible Societies
are issuing reports on what they do (and I want to
add that our mission enjoys very cordial relationships
with the major Bible societies generally).

But this is the way it so often works: in
Romania, for instance, quite a number of Bible
copies have been printed, though in a translation
totally unacceptable for evangelical Protestants—in
fact, not even available for Protestants. Now, notice
this statement in an official report: ". . . the
distribution of Scriptures is being carried out through
the congregations which have been offered a
number of Scriptures proportionate to the numerical
strength"—and then says that on the average each
Romanian Orthodox church in the past four years
has received 21 copies of the Bible. And there's
another catch revealed in the report: "Send full lists
of purchasers to the patriarchate together with
payment in funds. . . ." That means that everyone
who got a Bible is now registered as possessing a
Bible. This is one of the things we are strongly
against, because in many other countries this policy
has brought about numerous arrests.

There is another very touchy point that cannot
be ignored. Many tourists have come back to the
West with glowing reports about the fervent crowds
that jam the services in the Moscow Baptist church.

What they don't seem to comprehend is that the Communist regime tolerates that "showcase church" as a token of Soviet religious freedom specifically to put visitors' minds at rest about the reports of persecution. The truth needs to be told.

In the Soviet Union in 1960, the official council of the evangelical church in Moscow issued a decree that included a few points utterly disagreeable to the evangelical leaders in the rest of the country. It ruled that it was not permissible to preach any more evangelistic sermons, or to give an altar call, or to let children attend the meetings. Also, they had to reduce greatly the number of young people being baptized; the age limit was already 18, but even that had to be cut down, and no more people over 18 could be baptized unless they were the very old.

Men of God such as Kropofiev, and Vins, and Kryuchkov, protested: "No, we cannot do that. You go too far in cooperating with the Communist regime. We have to break away."

This started the "Initiative Church," sometimes referred to as the unregistered church (wrongly called "the underground church"). This unregistered Evangelical Baptist Church, since August, 1961, has witnessed such astounding growth that today we estimate its membership in Russia to be about three times as large as the official registered church.

When William Tolbert, a former president of the Baptist World Alliance, now the president of Liberia, visited Moscow (of course, he did not visit the unregistered church although it was a much bigger movement) he made an official statement about the Initiative Church: "It is a mistake to follow this way. The laws of the state regarded by Christians as directed against their interests and disagreeable to them for this reason, must nevertheless be observed."

I strongly disagree. We must *not* obey the law of the government if it is directed against the interests of the Christians. We have another allegiance, and that is to Jesus Christ.

Well, we say it was terrible for the official Baptist church to compromise with the government, and now to be literally persecuting other believers. But if those people had not done that, then today the true church would be much smaller. As so often before in history, out of evil God still works good— and we should be encouraged that this has happened.

False powers allowed to test us
That whole situation, however, does emphasize the highly dangerous potential that a "super-church," if such a concept has any real meaning, is going to

be a church that persecutes its own saints with the cooperation of the government. No church can thrive, or even survive indefinitely, if it tries to play games with governments according to Godless rules.

I find another observation by Dr. Dotsenko to be very helpful in this connection. He says that "God allows . . . false powers to operate to test our faithfulness to him, to check our worth for the eternal life."

He goes on: "No true power has a right to intervene in the worship of God and Christ as it is prescribed in the Scriptures. Christians ought to obey all laws that do not make them turn away from worshiping and serving God and Christ . . . To accept the leadership of Communists is incompatible with the true service of God. It is like accepting the assertion that the thief is the lawful owner of the things he stole."

For the student of God's Word, hostility toward the church of Jesus Christ comes as no surprise. The Bible makes it very clear that the nations of this world simply are not for Christ. In Luke 21, where Jesus gives his sermon on the end time, describing earthquakes, famines, pestilences, terrors and great signs from heaven, he says: "But before all this they will lay their hands on you and persecute you, delivering you up to the synagogues and prisons, and you will be brought before kings and governors for my name's sake."

Jesus is saying here that persecution is carried out by people, but in the name of the government. It's governments that run the prisons, and this verse implies that the government may even run the church. There you see again how wrong this world is, how it is indeed turned upside down! It surely is time that we come along and put it right.

Then our Lord goes on to say: "You will be delivered up even by parents and brothers and kinsmen and friends." This has literally happened in Russia. One of the "saints" of Soviet youth is Pavlik Morozov, a young boy who betrayed his father and his uncles to execution when they tried to save their families from starvation by not giving 95 percent of their crops to Communist authorities. But it was not that boy who killed his father; it was the government.

Finally Jesus says: "You will be hated by all for my name's sake. . . By your endurance you will gain your lives" (or, "While you endure it, you will gain your life"). This verse on perseverance and endurance is in relation to the government, not to other things that you have thought till now. We often take it out of its context, and tell our young converts, "If you endure to the end, you will be saved."

But the point there is the pressures of the government upon the church of Christ. Karl Barth, that great Swiss theologian, said something like this: "A government always tends to move between two extremes. It's either Romans 13—servant of God; or it is on the other end, Revelation 13—the beast that came out of the sea and out of the earth."

What does Revelation 13:10 say? "If anyone is to be taken captive, to captivity he goes; if anyone slays with the sword, with the sword he must be slain."

The call is for endurance and faith of the saints. Jesus foresaw that the church is going through a time just like that which he went through when he died on the cross of Calvary.

The enemies of God

After all of this discussion, it may occur to someone to ask: What about those Scriptures that say we are to love our enemies and to pray for them?

Yes, what about those?

Dr. Dotsenko says: "The true enemies of the Christian are those who are the enemies of God. All other people are his brothers and sisters in Christ. These he should love and forgive. Concerning the enemies of God, only one prayer is possible: that the Lord in his mercy will open their eyes and soften their hearts so that they will repent and accept Christ as their Lord and Savior."

That insight helps me understand a verse that I always had problems with, Psalm 139:21: "Do not I hate them, O Lord, that hate thee?" The Bible never tells us that we must love God's enemies. We must love only our enemies because they are on a horizontal level, and at that level, we never really know who is right and who is wrong. Both can be wrong, or both can be right, and still be quarreling.

Where God's enemies are involved, however, it is not a matter of their being my enemies and of my leaving it to Almighty God to decide who is right or wrong. There it's clear that they are wrong —they are God's enemies—and nowhere in the Bible is there any injunction that I must love those who hate God. We must not hate people, but we must not love the God-haters.

Can you see more clearly now the true spiritual nature of this battle that engages all of our energies? When we oppose and fight the anti-God (and anti-human) decrees and regulations of atheistic political systems such as Communism, we actually are waging a battle against the powers of darkness that Satan has unleashed on this earthly scene from that invisible world of the spirit where he is

frantically trying to stave off his doom that was
secured in the glorious victory of Jesus Christ.

The silent majority too silent
One more thing my heart constrains me to say on
this tremendous subject. When I read Isaiah 42:22,
I seem to see my brothers and sisters in Christ
living under Communist oppression today:

"But this is a people robbed and plundered,
they are all of them trapped in holes and hidden in
prisons; they have become a prey with none to
rescue, a spoil with none to say, 'Restore.' "

For that phrase "to say" I want to substitute
"none to demand." None to approach the enemy,
the enemy of souls, and demand that he let my
people go, as Moses demanded of Pharoah, and as
Jesus came with the demand to the prince of
darkness. Let my people go!

Christians in the West generally are the silent
majority, making no such demand. Spineless,
colorless, passive individuals, we as the silent
majority form the bridge over which the world of
corruption, revolution and hatred passes
unhindered. Passes over to corrode and curse the
lives of the rising generations. And in what we call
democracy there is no force that can possibly stop
it, except the power of God.

He really has to be made manifest in us. The big problem in our democracies is that we even have liberty to kill democracy, and we are working real hard on it by being the silent majority in our own nations, not defending the liberties of our own families, and not speaking out for those who have no democracy—who cannot speak without going to prison or to death for it.

None to *demand*—Restore!

Is this what God has to say about the church today? About the silent majority?

In not speaking out for the persecuted church, in not taking our stand for Jesus Christ, we *fully* back the devil in his evil plans for exterminating the church today.

You see, there is no way to avoid involvement in the spiritual warfare. If we say nothing, and do nothing, our very default becomes a major contribution to the triumph of Godlessness. On the other hand, if we act aggressively in obedience to Christ's command, and in reliance on the mighty spiritual resources which God makes available, we shall see the very gates of hell give way!

Jesus is King of kings and Lord of lords. He shall reign forever and ever. What a destiny is ours to be marching in his train across the battlefield which is this world!

3

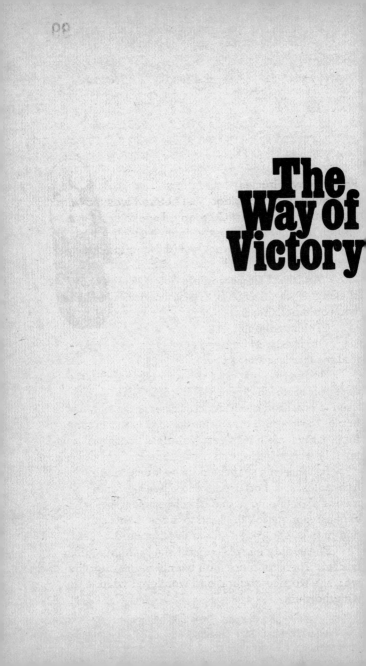

The Way of Victory

Present-day miracles

One Sunday not long ago, just before I was leaving on another trip to East Germany, I spoke at a large church in Holland and asked intercession for that venture. After the meeting, a slightly agitated lady approached me.

"Andrew, I know you are going to Germany," she said. "Now, I have a very bad conscience. I wish you could help me."

"Tell me about it."

Obviously under deep conviction of sin, she told me this touching story.

During and just after the war, she lived in the east part of Holland near the German border, and used to entertain the American officers there in her home. They would then bring textiles to her and her family. Such cloth was very valuable because it was terribly scarce in Holland at that time.

Because she suspected those men probably had stolen it, or had used some other improper means of obtaining it, and also because it was such expensive material, the kind to make men's suits and linings, she kept it stored in cardboard boxes.

The supply increased until she had quite a big box full. Then, for more than twenty years after the war, she worried about it and wondered what to do with the stuff.

On that Sunday morning when I spoke in her church, the Lord got through to her.

"Andrew," she asked, "can you please take this to Germany and just give it to some Germans? It will relieve my conscience to know that, to the best of my knowledge, it has gone back to where it should be."

I told her I would do that.

The next weekend, I loaded my station wagon with all the things that I wanted to take across the border. Then, without thinking it over further, I simply put with my luggage the big box of textiles that she had sent to me after that Sunday.

When I came to the West German border, the officer said, "Do you have anything to declare, sir?"

Realizing that I was in Germany, I replied, "No, sir," and then added to myself, "not to you."

The next morning I arrived at the East German border. Again, that same question from the guard: "Do you have anything to declare?"

"Yes," I answered, "a lot!"

"What?"

I opened the rear of my station wagon.

"Here," I said, "is a box full of textiles that I want to take into the country."

"What are you going to do with it?"

"I will give it away."

"To whom?"

"I don't know."

Well, that really brought the question marks to his face! So I added, "I can explain it to you, sir."

I gave him the story of what had happened the previous Sunday morning, but I extended it a little so that it became a full-fledged sermon on restitution and the need for forgiveness and a clean heart, and God's forgiveness. Of course, I used the story of the lady, but I made it just a little longer to get the gospel across to the officer there at the border.

All this time, he had a deeply puzzled look on his face. He turned to me.

"Sir," he said, "I'll have to talk it over inside my office, because I never had a case like this at the border."

Well, I thought, he probably hadn't!

He went inside, and twenty minutes passed before he came out again. He had talked to all the superiors in the office, and still came up with no answer.

"Tell me again," he inquired, "to whom are you going to give it?"

"Honestly," I said, "I do not know and I do not care." Then I asked: "Do you want it?"

"Oh, no, I can't do that."

"Well, all right. I just want to give it to somebody."

"Where?"

"I don't know. I am going to be traveling all over the country. Listen, if you don't know what to do and I can't pass with all of this, you may seal it and I'll just take it into West Berlin and give it away to German people there. But this lady did receive it from Germany, and she wants me to give it to someone in Germany. That's all."

Again, he had that deeply perplexed look. He went back into the office and phoned, probably all the way to East Berlin to some office. He didn't know what to do. After a long, long time, he came out to me again and just shrugged his shoulders.

"Sir, just take it, go, and give it to anybody you want."

He never asked me about anything else to declare. But I had told him the truth. When he asked if there was anything to declare, I had answered truthfully and had shown him one box. He became nonplussed by my lengthy explanation—and who knows what God may have done in his heart, anyway.

So he let me just pass. They'd never had such a thing happen before. Usually if you had so much as a dollar's worth you had to declare it. I had

hundreds of dollars' worth, and no written
declaration, and he let me take it in to give it away
to whomever I chose.

I call that a miracle!

There's a second part to the story. Later in the
afternoon, I drove into the city and went to the home
of a tailor with whom I usually stayed. There I found
a young Hungarian lady whom I'll call Anna. She
was the daughter of a Baptist pastor who served as
my interpreter in Hungary. I had brought the two
families in touch with each other. First they became
pen pals, and later they exchanged visits.

"What are you doing here, Anna?" I asked in
surprise.

"As you know," Anna explained, "my parents
are very poor." (I well knew! I had worked a great
deal with her father, who ministered among Gypsies
in Hungary. He is a real man of God, thrown out of
the ministry because of distributing Russian Bibles
to the troops. It brought great poverty.)

"My mother sent me to East Germany to try to
find some textile to make a suit for my daddy."

Well, I thought I was in heaven! Such clear
guidance. Every little detail in place—truth prevail-
ing and God's power so evident. Guidance given to
every one involved, including the Communists and
people in East Germany, the tailor, and the fine Bap-

tist pastor in Hungary, and this girl arriving at this time on the opposite side of the very same errand that brought me there. It was marvelous!

Because I was in the house of a tailor, I could cut off just enough of the cloth for this man's suit, or a couple of them, and the rest I could still give away to other people who needed it.

There's still another chapter to tell about that trip, but first I want to emphasize yet another principle about this spiritual warfare that the Lord Jesus has ordered us to wage in his Name. Because he holds all authority in heaven and on earth, and because his hosts surround us with their power in the invisible world, we who are obedient to him can expect with full confidence that our Almighty God will bring his purposes to pass through nothing less than miracles!

What is a miracle? Let me give you my definition: a miracle is the sovereign act of God based on Truth. The Truth! Truth on my part, of course, in the conviction that God *is* Truth. When truth and Truth meet, then God performs miracles.

There are no small miracles, by the way. Every miracle is big, whether you get a penny when you need a penny, or a million dollars when you need that. The miracle as such is equally large in both cases. No difference there, because a miracle is

God's act based on Truth. And it doesn't happen
only at the Communist border, but *anywhere* and
anytime for *anyone* who is faithful in the Lord's
service.

Too many lions in midair
There are some people, I know, who say it's all a
matter of coincidence. I heard a story about an
American college professor who was ridiculing
students who believed the account in 2 Kings 19
where the Assyrians laid siege in Judah. God said:
"I will defend this city to save it, for my own sake
and for the sake of my servant David." Then, in
the night, the Lord smote 185,000 in the camp of the
Assyrians, and the men of Judah arose in the
morning to find all those dead bodies.

The college professor called this a coincidence.
A young man protested, saying it was God
delivering his people, God's guidance, and all that.

"Now listen," said the professor, "if you walk
in a jungle and all of a sudden a lion begins to jump
at you, and as he is flying through midair a coconut
drops from a tree and lands on the head of the lion
and knocks him out so you can escape, would you
call that coincidence or guidance?"

The student thought for a while, with everybody
staring at him. Then he replied, "Well, I might call

that coincidence. But if I walk in the jungle and all of
a sudden 185,000 lions jump at me and as they are
all in midair, ready to land on me, at that moment
185,000 coconuts dropped on their heads, then I
would not call that coincidence. I would call it
guidance or God's mighty intervention!"

I think that student won his argument.

I tell people that if I take Bibles across a border
once and something remarkable happens, you might
call it a coincidence. But I have been doing that for
eighteen years, full time, with all my teams, and
always something happens that distracts the guards'
attention, or just makes us think that they haven't
even seen us or seen our load. You cannot possibly
call that coincidence. It's God's miraculous guidance
and intervention!

To advance the cause of Christ
But God is not a prankster, who does wonderful
things just to show off his power. Every miracle of
God is worked for the purpose of advancing the
cause of Jesus Christ against the opposition of the
enemy, and for bearing witness to the gospel,
directly or indirectly. Let me go back now to that
story of my trip into East Germany with the textiles.

Later I headed back home from Berlin through
the 100-mile Russian-occupied zone of East Germany

to West Germany. I had been working in the refugee
camps with a Dutch theologian, a tall young fellow,
and we had been giving out Scriptures to the people
from different countries and languages. I had a load
of Bibles left in eastern European languages which I
was taking back with me in my VW to Holland
where I could repack them, and then take them
myself or send them or have other teams take them
to the eastern European countries later.

I had not hidden them. I just had all this in
cardboard boxes because so far I had never
encountered any problems at the East German
border between Berlin and West Germany. This time
as I stopped there at Helmstadt, an officer came up
to my car and pointed to one of the cardboard boxes.

"What's in there?"

With a very big smile, I said: "Sir, there are
Bibles in that box."

He frowned.

"Take the box into my office," he ordered.

We did. We carried the heavy box into his
office and put all the books on tables. We filled three
tables with New Testaments, Gospels, and complete
Bibles in various eastern European languages,
including German.

He checked every book to see where it was
printed. I was lucky they weren't printed in New

York; they were all from Sweden, Germany, Switzerland and Holland, so that passed.

"Do you have anything else?" he asked.

Again I smiled, and said, "Yes, sir. I have a lot more."

He marched back to my vehicle, right to the back of the VW, and pointed to a box.

"What's in there?"

"Flannelgraph stories."

"What's that?"

I have developed a habit of making very long sentences, so as to get the gospel across in every sentence. A guard has to listen to at least one sentence if he asks me a question! That way I can tell about Jesus.

"Well, sir," I responded, "they are flannelgraph stories that teachers use to tell children about the Lord Jesus Christ, because even children can believe on him, because when a child is old enough to love his parents he can love Jesus who came into the world to save sinners so that children as well as grown-up people by simple faith in him can have eternal life and go to heaven when they die."

That was my sermonette in a sentence!

He left the box right there, but he pulled out one of the folders and opened it in my car. I was embarrassed because it was a map of the Mediterra-

nean, with the travels of the Apostle Paul marked
with dots and lines, and all the countries, seas, and
islands identified. It looked like a proper spy map!

Looking at me very crossly, he said: "Aha! You
said it was for little children—"

"Yes, sir," I interrupted, "it's just a map of the
travels of the Apostle Paul who first of all came to
Europe to tell about the Lord Jesus Christ so that we
in Europe should hear about the great message of
Jesus Christ, and if he had not come here we would
still be barbarians living without God—practically
as atheists."

That was my second sermonette.

He really got cross with me then.

"Take it into my office!"

We did.

We saw that the office was full of Red soldiers
picking up those beautiful books, trying to read the
Word of God. When I put the box down, more
people flowed into that hall—Red Army soldiers
and officers.

He pulled another folder from my box—and
again, it was the worst possible one he could have
chosen. It was the story of Ephesians 6: the whole
armor of God! When he opened it, out fell the sword
and the helmet and all the rest. It looked very
dangerous for me.

Again that angry look on his face, and he
mumbled something more about children.

"Really, it is!" I insisted. "I can't explain it, but
let me demonstrate it."

I asked my friend Anton to hold the background
of black cloth. He was very tall, 6'6", and held it
back against the wall. I took a figure of an
undressed boy and stuck it to the flannel
background, and began to tell the story.

"Here is a man in the world, unprotected from
sin and demons and sickness and darkness and
disease. He needs protection. Man cannot live
without God . . ."

I put on him the helmet of salvation.

"You've got to believe in the Lord Jesus Christ
to be saved and know that you have eternal life."

Then I quickly put on him the breastplate of
righteousness.

". . . because you have to live a righteous life,
and all these Godless people in this world make a
mess of it and murder people . . ." I gave the story,
of course, about Hitler's Nazi Germany. ". . . and
now we can't allow that to happen because people
living without God bring the whole world into
bondage . . ."

Then I put the shield of faith in the little
figure's hand and said that with faith we are pro-

tected. "Whatever happens in the world, if we have personal faith through salvation in our heart, we live a holy life and we have the shield of faith so that all the onslaughts of the enemy, all the attacks, can be thwarted right here with the shield of faith . . ."

I was just going to grab the sword and put it in his hand and speak about the Word of God, when it dawned on the man that I was preaching to them! Well, I had a captive audience—the office was filled with soldiers and officers—and of course I spoke in German. When he found out that I was preaching, he was furious.

"Now stop this! Put it all back in your boxes and take it to your car and go!

"No, sir," I said. "I would like to give each of you a souvenir. I somewhat enjoyed being with you so long."

I got out a pile of John's Gospels and tried to hand them out. They couldn't possibly accept them. They put their hands behind their backs and marched away, leaving Anton and me to take the Bibles and flannelgraph stories back to the car— and we drove away!

A double-barreled prayer

With God working miracles, we don't have to try to outsmart the guards at border crossings. I am determined not to tell a lie, but I pray mighty hard that I won't have to tell the truth either. That may sound like an impossible contradiction, so let me explain.

I said earlier that Godless men who have given themselves over to the service of the devil and his forces do not any longer have a right to the truth. After all, their allegiance is to the one whom Jesus called a liar and the father of lies. As a matter of fact they are not even interested in the truth—and probably don't recognize it when it stares them in the face.

Now there are several ways that I come at this matter of the truth in dealing with the enemy. Remember, we who love the Lord are in the service of the truth, and know that it is the basis on which God works his miracles. So I want to stress again what I have said before: I do not lie.

For one thing, I believe in the *concealment* of the truth. Here's an illustration of how that works.

One Sunday morning, a Christian boy was going to one of the secret house meetings of believers behind the Iron Curtain. Everyone knew that the police were trying to find out where the church was meeting, so his father warned him that day to be very careful to watch out for the police.

All alone, the boy made his way quietly

toward the meeting house. Christians had to go one at a time. Other members of the family would have to go at different times and take different approaches to the meeting place. I have practiced this myself in going to such meetings in Communist countries.

Walking along happily, he suddenly was stopped by police who had been hiding behind a tree.

"Stop!" they ordered. "Where are you going?"

The boy stood there for a moment, determined not to tell a lie, but probably equally determined not to tell the truth. He must have shot a telegram prayer to heaven (which the Lord answers providing you take proper time for prayer when you have the time!).

He looked the policeman in the eye and with a very sad face (sad because he had been caught!) he lowered his voice for reply:

"Sir, I am going to see my brothers and sisters. This morning we are going to open the testament of my oldest brother."

The policeman took pity on him and said, "All right, sonny, on you go!"

This boy had really saved the situation for the church. He had not told a lie, but had told the truth in concealment, inasmuch as he was dealing with an enemy who was not entitled to know the truth.

Jesus used this same method to conceal truth from the Pharisees and leaders who were enemies of God. "And as soon as He was alone, His followers, along with the twelve, began asking Him about the parables. And He was saying to them, 'To you has been given the mystery [secret] of the Kingdom of God; but those who are outside get everything in parables; in order that while seeing, they may see and not perceive; and while hearing, they may hear and not understand . . .' " (Mark 4:10-12, NASB).

The enemies of God were already sinning against truth which they understood. If they were told more truth it would mean more condemnation. God, in grace, mercy, and love, does not want them to know certain things lest their judgment be even greater.

Some border guards and policemen seem not to want more knowledge at times for the same reason. They do not want to be responsible for even more rebellion against truth, God, and God's people—in short, the Kingdom of God!

Jesus showed mercy to King Herod in Luke 23:9, for Herod "questioned (Jesus) at some length but (Jesus) answered him nothing."

This is different from what is known as "situational ethics," which says that a person may do immoral things (adultery, lying, stealing) if the situation demands it (e.g., to save his life or freedom). I am not saying that, but rather the opposite. I am saying we must always obey God's truth. It never changes, although sinners may change and so may their rules and laws, especially when sin and their battle against truth and God's Kingdom increase. Our heart's intent and acts of the will must always be truthful in God's eyes, although people committed to Satan's kingdom will not perceive it.

Charles Finney said, "To withhold truth for a good motive cannot be considered sin."

To obey God is always to have the right motive. We have God and angels to save our lives or help us escape from prison when he sees it is best for his Kingdom.

No peaceful coexistence

In dealing with people—individuals or groups, even nations and governments—when mutual understanding is one of the relevant or requisite considerations, then and only then are we under obligation to do our utmost to ensure that what we say or what we do is not concealed. In that case, you see, they have a claim to the truth.

But our enemy never has a claim to the truth,

nor has the border guard who is in his service. I am under no obligation whatsoever to tell him what I am concealing, because I am engaged in a spiritual warfare and we never talk things over with our enemy!

Consider Matthew 28 again. Jesus said: "Go into all the world and proclaim the gospel." He didn't say that we must have a conference with the enemy. Jesus himself did not have a conference with the devil to try to settle their dispute by a common agreement.

The word "dialogue" is much too fashionable today. You cannot have a dialogue with your enemy—not in the realm of the spirit. Jesus had no such dialogue with the devil.

Our Lord commands us to go and proclaim. Defeat the enemy. Rescue those who are perishing under the dominion of sin and Satan. Once you know this, you know that when you get to the border crossing you are in *God's* business. It's none of the enemy's business to know what you are doing. You conceal it. He has no right to know the truth.

You don't have to tell a lie, either. Just have faith in God that he will see you through, and then go on with the business. Because the enemy has utterly forfeited any right to know the truth, very

often concealment is an obligation which the truth
itself requires.

Nor does that mean that you must hate the
persons. We must always bear in mind that they
serve their master—usually better than we serve
ours! So we are fighting against that wicked lord,
or his ideas, or the ideology which has caught that
man in its error, not directly against the man
himself. Under all circumstances, we should look
for a chance to share with such a man the saving
truth of the gospel of Jesus Christ which will deliver
him into the realm and service of truth if he will
accept it.

Leaving out some part

Along with concealment, there is also a principle of
partial truth, which is not to be mistaken for untruth.
In Exodus 1 is an interesting example. The midwives
of the Hebrews were ordered to kill all the baby
boys born to Jews (no one demanded that the
mothers themselves do it). They didn't obey the
order. So the king of Egypt called the midwives and
said, "Why have you done this, and let the male
children live?"

Listen to their answer.

The midwives said, "Because the Hebrew
women are not like the Egyptian women; for they

are vigorous and are delivered *before* the midwife comes to them."

What is this? For one thing, it's speaking the truth. Modern doctors know that a pregnant woman will have an easier delivery if she keeps moving and does exercises. But if she sits in a chair or lies in bed all those months, her delivery is likely to be more difficult.

The Hebrew women in Egypt had to work hard. They were slaves and they were exploited. It was terrible, but it kept them so healthy and strong that the midwives didn't have much to do there. Of course, the baby had arrived before the call came through.

So here we have an instance of what I call "partialities." The Bible makes clear why the midwives disobeyed Pharaoh's command: "because the midwives feared God" (verse 21). They concealed the whole truth by telling only "partial truth." The Hebrew mothers were quick; the midwives got there, of course, but they were not going to destroy the baby after it was born. That part they withheld from Pharaoh's knowledge. What they said was the truth—in part, and it saved their lives by throwing enough sand in his eyes so that he couldn't see any farther.

Just to review another basic principle of this

spiritual warfare: notice that the midwives disobeyed Pharaoh, the legal authority, because they feared God. Remember, we either break God's commands and stick to our own silly manmade superpious traditions, or we break our traditions and become vital Christians in the way that Jesus and the apostles were. Not fearing Pharaoh, not fearing the enemy, but obeying God: the choice is ours.

Inspired interpretation

Another useful employment of the truth is *interpretation*. While there is no law that Bibles should not be imported into Communist countries, there is a law that you have to declare all the goods that you have. I tell you, it can be pretty tricky at times.

I had taken several loads of Scriptures into the Soviet Union and never had any trouble. I did not exactly put them on display, but I took them in anyway. One day I came with a load of 800 Bibles, plus thousands of tracts. I knew that on the other side were hundreds of pastors, and I'd promised them I would give every one his own Bible.

The Russians, however, came up with a new idea at the border. They had a big form for me to fill out. One of the questions was: "Are you taking into the Soviet Union any literature, written or printed, that could do damage to the political and economic situation of the Soviet Union?"

I admit that I was pinned down at that moment. So I decided to change some money, and get my insurance papers ready, and all that in order to gain some time—because I couldn't fill that out; I couldn't sign that I was not doing it. I had 800 Bibles and thousands of tracts!

Quietly I prayed: "Lord God, give me light. I want to obey you, only you, no one else. There are people praying for a Bible and I am going to be the answer to their prayer, yet I am not going to tell a lie. Help me! What can I do?"

I knew I couldn't back out. I could not simply turn the car around and run back into that other Iron Curtain country, Poland, because then they would probably say, "Why didn't you go farther?"

I had to find a way out. As I prayed, the Lord gave me an idea. He said: "Andrew, you're not going to sell those Bibles on the black market (they could bring two or three hundred dollars apiece) and become a millionaire overnight, so you are not going to do any damage to the economic situation. You are going to give them to believers. You are not going to give them to Brezhnev or Khrushchev (who were still there at that time) or Kosygin or any other Communist party leaders. You are going to give them to the pastors who need tools to lead Russians to Christ. So you are not going to do violence to the political situation. It's not *against* the political situation; it's only *for* the Kingdom of God."

I found peace in my heart. I took my pen and signed the paper. God had given me the interpretation that satisfied my heart.

Of course, I realized that if they should find the Bibles after I had signed the declaration, they would come up with a different interpretation and I would be in for trouble. But I felt sure that I could risk it. I knew that the God who identified himself with Peter in prison, and with Daniel's three friends in the fiery furnace, was the God who identified himself with me because I was not going to comply with the enemy's demands to declare the Bibles and in that way lose them.

Truth contingent on change

The truth can be understood also with reference to circumstances of *change*. When conditions are altered, or your companions or your opponents change, then you consequently have to change behavior, attitude, sometimes even words that have been promised, because they become void on account of the altered situation.

Consider the approach Moses made to

Pharaoh (Exodus 5): "We just want to make a three days' journey into the wilderness to sacrifice, and then we will be back." He even sets certain limitations on who is going to join him, not the whole nation but just some. And he will be back, he said.

But Pharaoh cheated on Moses and in the end, of course, he didn't let them go. After the resultant plagues, Pharaoh finally did let Moses go—with all the wives, children, cattle and all their possessions.

What happened in that sequence of events? Originally, in the first request, Moses said, "It is a three-day journey, and we will be back. . . ." But now that he is at last leaving Egypt, he knows very well he will never be back—and he didn't promise that to Pharaoh, either! Because Pharaoh, through the months of negotiations, changed his attitude, hardened his heart; therefore there was a change of plans and of behavior in Moses which he didn't care to reveal to Pharaoh. When the children of Israel did eventually pull out of Egypt, they never came back. The truth was contingent on the circumstantial changes.

Remember the story of Jonah's preaching mission to Nineveh? He told them that because of their sins, God would destroy their city in forty days. But God never did destroy it. Why not? Did God change his mind? He surely did, because the people met his conditions by repenting. The situation changed because their behavior changed—so God's word changed.

A quite remarkable example of this appears in the life of our Lord Jesus himself. In John 7, we read: "After this, Jesus went about in Galilee; he would not go about in Judea, because the Jews sought to kill him."

Wait a minute! Which Jews? The government. Don't forget—please don't forget it—Jesus came as an invader from another kingdom. He came as another king, opposed to King Herod and the whole religious, political, and economic system of that time. He came on behalf of another kingdom, to establish it. Consequently, all the governments were against him.

Is it any different today?

The Jews wanted to kill Jesus. Does he just walk overnight into their trap? The Feast of Tabernacles was at hand, and Jesus' brothers urged him to go to Judea so his works could be displayed openly for all to see. A man who wants to be known, they told him, doesn't work in secret.

Who says so? Jesus worked partly in secret and partly in the open. They were trying to force him out of the pattern he had established for his ministry.

He replies: "My time has not yet come, but your time is always here."

In other words, Jesus is implying that if you always agree with the local government, then you can always do what you want, because you cooperate or give in to their wishes and thus you don't get into trouble. That's one sure way to avoid persecution: always agree with your government—good or bad.

Then the Lord says (verse 8): "Go to the feast yourselves; I am not going up to this feast." Hear that? "I am *not* going up to this feast, for my time has not yet fully come." So saying, he remained in Galilee.

But after his brothers had gone up to this feast (verse 10), *then he also went!* Not publicly, but in private—or in secret, as other versions have it.

Jesus even disobeyed government orders on the resurrection morning by rolling away the stone which was sealed with a government seal and guarded by soldiers.

Jesus working in secret? Jesus going underground? Jesus disobeying government orders? Could it be so? If he sets this precedent, shouldn't some of his followers do the same?

In John 12, Jesus gives the principle involved here. He says to the people (verse 35): "The light is with you for a little longer. Walk while you have the light, lest the darkness overtake you; he who walks in the darkness does not know where he goes. While you have the light, believe in the light, that you may become sons of light." After Jesus said this, "he departed and hid himself from them."

That's strange. It seems to be a contradiction. Jesus says that there's light, so walk in the light—and Jesus goes into darkness, into hiding.

What did Jesus say? Walk while you *have* the light. There comes a time (John 9:4) when night comes, and then no man can work. Jesus says that there comes a time when we don't have the light, don't have the liberty to go and witness for him. Then, he says, we will have to change our actions and change our attitude. A change in behavior comes in response to a certain development.

Things change. Government may change. Instead of a democratically chosen government, we may get dictatorship. Then our actions will greatly change. The truth demands that we act in accordance with the relevant facts and relevant conditions. When they change, our action changes accordingly.

Just one more simple illustration of this: When Jesus meets the centurion who has a paralyzed servant (Matthew 8), he says he will come and heal him. But when the centurion gave his great testimony

to the authority of Jesus that could heal by giving
the word only, Jesus changed his plans, and did *not*
go to the house, and yet he healed the servant.

Biblical ethics regarding the strategies of war
and truthfulness is not always concerned with
words, but sometimes with actions and other forms
of signification. I call it a strategy of *opposing
forces* when we employ action intended to deceive
the enemy.

In all the work we do in Communist countries,
we don't have to tell *them* our moves. We do have
to inform our prayer partners about some of our
program; but as to our real strategy, we don't tell
even our prayer partners everything because we
don't want to give away our trade secrets. Far less
likely are we to publish our strategy and make it
known to our enemy.

Furthermore, it's a part of the strategy to take
actions which deceive the enemy without our having
to tell a lie in words. Again, we have a biblical
illustration of that. In Joshua 8, the Hebrews are
expecting to conquer Ai, the second city in
Canaan, as easily as they had just captured Jericho.
But something went wrong. Because there was a
traitor in the camp, a thief, they lost the first battle
and many lives.

Then we read: "The Lord said to Joshua,

'Stretch out the javelin that is in your hand toward Ai, for I will give it into your hand" (8:18). What had Joshua heard from the Lord before? To lie in ambush in order to conquer the city. But now he was to retreat, what I call "designed and feigned retreat" or "simulated defeat."

Joshua was under no obligation, of course, to inform the enemy that the retreat he made was not real. It was just a maneuver to get the people out so that the other army which he had hidden around the corner could then come in, set fire to the city, and cause a panic so that they could destroy the whole army. Joshua didn't have to tell that to the captains of Ai. This was the strategy of war! The people of Ai failed to see through Joshua's plan and were self-deceived by his apparent retreat.

The truth, then, is the Christian's best weapon against the enemy, because it is the basis upon which the Lord works miracles in answer to believing prayers. As I have been saying, we can employ the truth in many ways without telling our enemy what he has no right or business to know. And we do not tell a lie.

Prayer for the right question

If I have my car loaded with Bibles as I arrive at the Russian border and they ask, "Do you have any

Bibles?," I'll just beam at them and smile and say,
"Yes, a lot!" Sure, I'll tell them; but I pray hard
before I go that they won't ask me *that* question
but others instead. Or I pray that I may be able to
distract their thoughts and attention. It is remarkable
how the Lord just arranges for "little" things to
happen at the border.

One of our teams went to Bulgaria with a load
of Bibles in a huge pick-up van. Since it was
summer and we travel just like other tourists—which
we are, because we enjoy the sunshine and scenery
and swimming and all the rest—that group had an
inflatable canoe with them which I had bought and
often have with me when I take a trip there. They
had been lazy that day: after canoeing somewhere
in Yugoslavia, they didn't bother to let the air out.
So they squeezed the whole thing into the car and
drove off to the Bulgarian border with 700 Bibles
in the van.

At the border they gave their papers to one of
the officers while another, blissfully innocent, went
to the rear of the van and opened the door.

Pang! The canoe shot out the door right on his
head! He stood there for a moment, dizzy. Our boys
were very helpful; they ran to him and together
they pushed the canoe back into the car, locked
the door—and that was the end of the inspection.

Well, you could never arrange it that way or
do it a second time. It just happens. He could have
asked them to open the door and the canoe would
have hit them. But he didn't ask; he just opened
it himself!

Another team went to Czechoslovakia with
Bibles. Just before they reached the border, they
stopped for a last prayer meeting before crossing.
Being Dutch boys, they made themselves a cup of
coffee and opened a tin of milk. But, also because
they were boys, they forgot to put it away properly,
leaving the open tin on a box that was partly filled
with Bibles, partly with tools.

While they were in the office at the border
crossing having their papers checked, one of the
officers opened that big van and got inside to check
up on the luggage. Somehow he knocked over that
tin of condensed milk and spilled some on the floor.
He set it straight, jumped out of the vehicle and ran
to his office, got a cloth and ran back and began to
wipe it up. He apologized profusely and was ever so
sorry—and there was no more checking up
whatsoever! A tin of milk did that. It's always
something small that God uses in a big way.

Not long ago, I was returning from somewhere
and stayed overnight in a hotel in Germany.
Contrary to my usual practice, I had taken my

papers out and put them in a drawer in the desk there, because I had been writing in my hotel room every evening. When I left that place, I forgot all my papers in the drawer and didn't discover it until I was very close to the Dutch border.

What was I to do? I'll tell you: as a foreigner you might get into Holland without papers, but as a Dutchman you *cannot*. It is absolutely impossible at the border crossing; every Dutchman has to show his papers—car papers, passport, etc. You have never seen anybody get across without them.

I stood there in line with the other cars with my window open to the nice weather. Everybody was showing papers, and it went very quickly. There was the customs officer, and maybe just six feet to his right, and to my left, a painter was working. My turn was coming up next.

I was leaning out of the window and was already saying the first two words to the man: "I have—."

Just then, the painter said something funny to the customs officer. He turned to him and waved me through with his hand!

Just like that, no problem. I'm sure I was the only one that day or that week or that month who got through without showing papers. And it happened the very second I needed it. That is the

Lord's working! Otherwise, it would have cost me a lot of time and a lot of explanation to get through the border.

When I got home, again no problem: I phoned the hotel and asked them to send the papers by registered mail, and the next day I had them. The Lord always does that. For those people who still insist that such a way is not good, I just say: "Well, then, it means that the Lord is not calling you to do this." I think that should settle it.

Unwavering faith and trembling knees

I hope no one makes the mistake of concluding, in view of these incidents I've described, that this is an *easy* business. I cannot tell you how many times I have devoted myself to prayer and fasting to prove to myself and to the devil that I am willing to pay the price demanded. While it is wonderfully true that our victory has been assured in the Lord Jesus, we can never forget that the territory which we are commanded to invade is truly occupied right now by the enemy of Christ. I don't mind confessing that my knees tremble sometimes—but that doesn't make my faith waver.

Some critics object that our aggressiveness only makes things harder for the local believers we are trying to help. Well, I have two things to say to

that. First, in some places things could not be any
harder than they are already, and our coming in
and giving what help we can is the stimulus these
oppressed brothers need to keep hope alive and
courageous witnessing going forward. Second, I and
every worker in our mission know that we are to
sacrifice ourselves, even to death if need be, rather
than to do or say anything to incriminate local
believers and get them into trouble with the
authorities. After all, on the theological basis of
Galatians 2:20, we who have been once crucified
with Christ no longer need to give any thought to
"risk" of our lives.

What is so hard for outsiders to realize is that
those dear Christians in the Communist countries
literally are hazarding their lives for the gospel
every day; as I've said before, the records of
intimidation, persecution, imprisonment, torture and
execution are abundant, and constitute an
international scandal that even the United Nations
commissions seem helpless to do anything about.
We surely will not knowingly make their lot worse.

The moves we make to help them, it should be
remembered, are in response to their most intense
and prolonged pleadings for the very aid we bring.
We take every precaution to minimize the danger to
them, and do not go rushing into any situation

without receiving their careful instructions and without honoring their local arrangements. They, in turn, are deeply concerned not to jeopardize the effectiveness of our ministries. Together we labor to preserve and protect each other as we go about the Lord's business.

To meet the many needs, we supply much more than Bibles, precious and primary as they are. We provide food, clothing, and money in many cases of distress. For an evangelist in Romania, for instance, we provided a car to make his ministry more effective. For a brother in Yugoslavia, we gave money that would help purchase a building where he can hold Christian meetings without fear of arrest and imprisonment. Such is the specific assistance we have been enabled to give over and over again in the years of our labor. To preserve the local church and to extend its work is our reason for existence.

All this time that I am saying "we," I refer to scores of fellow-workers of mine who operate individually or as small teams, permanently or on a short-term basis, under the administration of our mission. This is not a one-man effort, although I seem to have been singled out for special publicity. While our International Headquarters is in my native Holland, the Open Doors mission has offices in the United States, Canada, England, New Zealand, South Africa, and the Philippines, with local officers and coordinators.

Since we have to function somewhat as a guerrilla movement, we try to keep our teams small, not more than twelve persons. This helps to prevent Communist infiltration, which is a constant threat and a reality in practically every Christian community. When one member gives evidence of special leadership gifts, he is encouraged to start a new group of his own. In one recent summer, the mission had fifty teams working in Europe.

The new testament way of doing it

As for this whole idea or concept of smuggling, which I still feel is a rather misleading term, it is probably *closest* to the whole New Testament concept of distributing the Word of God. In our Western nations, we enjoy the rare privilege of seeing people come to us for the message. We even wait for them to come. We put up special buildings for them to come into, and we open the doors, and welcome them with a smile.

In that connection, sometimes I feel that we've made a very wrong response to Jesus' announced intention to make us fishers of men. We have made a beautiful net (our church buildings) and have set it up on the shore waiting for the fish to jump in of their own accord!

In the first few hundred years of Christianity,
the believers never even owned a building. Our
experience of seeing people come to us, and of
waiting for them to come, is exactly the reverse flow
of the Great Commission. Because we have had it
this way for so long, we may even be starting to
question the right flow that God intended. What a
topsy-turvy world we live in!

A brother named George Young has said an
important word on this subject in a book called *The
Living Christ in Modern China.*

> The evangelism that we practice must be that
> healthy, balanced evangelism of Jesus. It seeks
> the salvation of the whole man—mind, body,
> and soul. Revival that we pray for must be
> spiritual and social. It must go deep in
> cleansing the moral life and widely transform
> the social and economic life of our nation. It
> must be a revival of apostolic preaching and
> apostolic practicing of Christianity. It is my
> deep personal conviction that the answer to
> the challenge of Communism is the re-birth of
> apostolic Christianity, with a flaming
> evangelism and the Kingdom of God
> community life which will be more
> revolutionary than that of the Communists.

That is the issue: that we have the courage, the Holy

Spirit boldness, to live a life that's more revolutionary than that of the Communists. The Lord will give us the insight to conduct raids, commando raids—call them hit-and-run! But we must go in and do something, for which we need nobody's permission —which, in fact, everybody will be against.

We do it because we know what we are doing. This world is enemy-occupied territory, filled with souls to whom Christ holds the rightful claim. Under his explicit command, we go in *by every possible means*—partial truth, concealment of truth, interpretation, change and opposition, or any other form of strategy that will help us to get in there with the gospel.

We are under obligation to obey God instead of men. His commandment is: *Go!* Whenever we dabble with this command, or compromise, or debate its morality, we simply deny God his right to rule the world. And that's exactly why the devil is in command.

It's time we stop this silly bickering and instead use Holy Spirit boldness to see the nations as God sees them. God has a plan, and he informs us. If Paul could be smuggled in and out, and if Peter did it, and if Jesus did it, and if God directed men like Elijah, Elisha, Joshua, Daniel and his friends, and Samuel on this issue, how much more will God give light today in this situation.

We are not facing an *ethical* issue but a
loyalty issue. If we are true followers of the Lord
Jesus Christ, we simply go into *all* the world because
he sends us. We need no welcome, we need no
invitation, we need no permission from the
government, we need no red-carpet treatment, we
need no VIP reception—unless it means Very
Important Prisoner for Christ's sake.

The command has been given by the risen Lord
and the issue is clear: *Spiritual battle!* Let's go in
Jesus' name, and *do* it! We *can* do it because ever
since he first issued the orders, Jesus has given to
every generation the ability, the strength, the
manpower, and the opportunity to do it.

Yet every generation has failed. The first
generation *almost* accomplished it. Almost! In our
generation we do not need to fail. We can fulfill the
commission, because Jesus Christ is the same
yesterday, today, and forever. He who holds all
authority in heaven and on earth has authorized us
to advance on his enemy everywhere, including
every Communist border crossing. He still endues
us with the power of the Holy Spirit in order to be
witnesses to the uttermost parts of the world.

"Awake, and strengthen what remains"
(Revelation 3:2).

That is the watchword of our ministry to

fellow-believers in eastern Europe and now in China as well. What constrains us is the love of Christ; for love, the Word of God tells us, is the fulfillment of all divine commands. I want others to have what makes me happy: *Jesus.* I want others to have what makes me grow spiritually: *The Bible.*

The God of miracles will bring it to pass!

For further literature, prayer letter,
and information, write to:
  Open Doors
  P. O. Box 2020
  Orange, California 92669
or directly to international headquarters:
  Brother Andrew
  Box 47
  Ermelo, Holland